FIRST 50 ROCK SONGS

YOU SHOULD PLAY ON ELECTRIC GUITAR

ISBN 978-1-4803-9808-5

HAL•LEONARD®
CORPORATION

7777 W. BLUEMOUND RD. P.O. BOX 13819 MILWAUKEE, WI 53213

Visit Hal Leonard Online at
www.halleonard.com

All Along the Watchtower

Words and Music by Bob Dylan

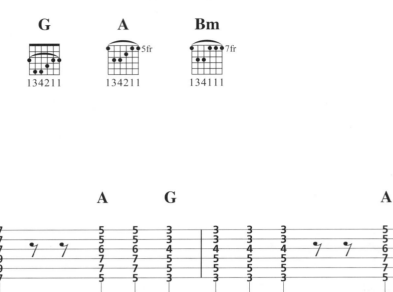

Key of Bm

Intro

Moderate Rock

w/ slight dist.

Play 4 times

𝄋 Verse

w/ Intro pattern

Bm		A	G		A Bm		A	G

1. "There must be some kind of way | out - ta here." | said the jok - er to the thief.
2., 3. *See additional lyrics*

	A Bm		A G		A Bm		A G

"There's too much con - fu - sion, | I can't get no re - lief.

	A Bm		A G		A Bm		A G

Busi - ness - men, they | drink my wine, | plow - men dig my earth.

	A Bm		A G		A Bm		A G

No rea - son to... | no - bod - y of it is worth.

To Coda 1 ⊕
To Coda 2 ⊕

Guitar Solo   *D.S. al Coda 1*

| A Bm | Bm | A G | A Bm | A Bm |

Hey!

⊕ **Coda 1**

Guitar Solo   *D.S. al Coda 2*

Play 7 times

‖: Bm | A G | A Bm :‖ Bm | A G | A Bm ‖

⊕ **Coda 2**

Outro-Guitar Solo

Play 7 times

‖: Bm | A G | A Bm :‖ Bm | A G | A Bm | ◇ ‖

Additional Lyrics

2. "No reason to get excited," the thief, he kindly spoke.
   "There are many here among us who feel that life is but a joke.
   Lord, but you and I, we been through that, and this is not our fate.
   So let us stop talkin' falsely now, the hour's getting late."

3. All along the watchtower, princes kept the view.
   While the women came and went, barefoot servants too.
   Outside in the cold distance, wildcats growl.
   Two riders were approaching and the wind began to howl!

All the Small Things

Words and Music by Tom De Longe and Mark Hoppus

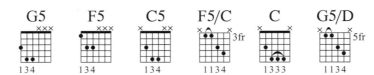

Key of C

Intro

Moderately fast

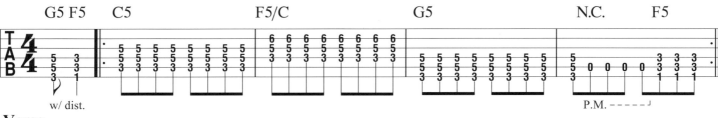

Verse

Pre-Chorus

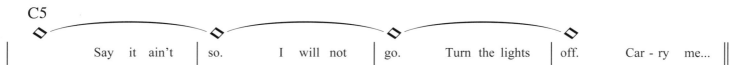

Chorus

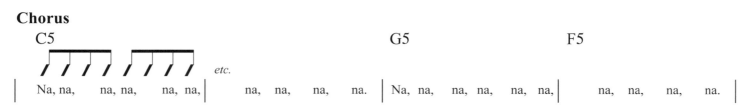

C5 | **G5** | **F5**

Na, na, na, na, na, na, | na, na, na, na. | Na, na, na, na, na, na, | na, na, na, na.

Interlude

w/ Intro pattern

| **C5** | **F5/C** | **G5** | **N.C.** **F5** |

D.S. al Coda

| **C5** | **F5/C** | **G5** | **N.C.** **F5** |

⊕ **Coda**

Interlude

C | **F5/C** | **G5/D** | *Play 4 times*

Outro

C5 | **G5** | **F5**

Say it ain't | so. I will not | go. Turn the lights | off. Car - ry me

C5 | **G5** | **F5**

home. Keep your head | still. I'll be your | thrill. The night will go | on, my lit - tle wind -

C5 | **G5** | **F5**

mill. Say it ain't | so. I will not | go. Turn the lights | off. Car - ry me

C5 | **G5**

home. Keep your head | still. I'll be your | thrill. The night will go |

F5 | **C5**

P.M. P.M. P.M. P.M.

on, the night will go | on, my lit - tle wind - | mill.

Basket Case

Words by Billie Joe
Music by Green Day

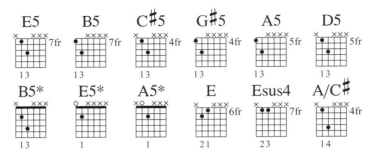

E5 B5 C#5 G#5 A5 D5
B5* E5* A5* E Esus4 A/C#

Tune down 1/2 step:
(low to high) Eb-Ab-Db-Gb-Bb-Eb

Key of E

Verse

Fast

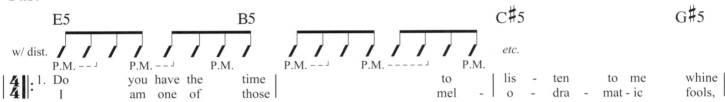

E5   B5   C#5   G#5

w/ dist.

P.M. --- | P.M. --- | P.M. | P.M. --- | P.M. ----- | P.M. *etc.*

4/4 | 1. Do   you have the   time   to   lis - ten   to me   whine |
     | I   am one   of   those   mel - o - dra - mat - ic   fools, |

                          A5   E5
     a - | bout   noth - ing and   ev |- 'ry - thing   all   at |
     neu - | rot - ic   to   the   bone,   no   doubt   a - bout   it. |

𝄋 Chorus

B5   A5 Some - times I   give   B5 my - self   the |
     once?   :|| Some - times I   give | my - self   the |

E5   A5   B5
     creeps.   Some - times my   mind | plays   tricks   on |

E5   A5   B5
     me.   It | all   keeps   add - ing   up. | I |

2nd time, To Coda 1 ⊕   *To Coda 2* ⊕

E5   D5   C#5   A5   B5

Pattern   **End Pattern**

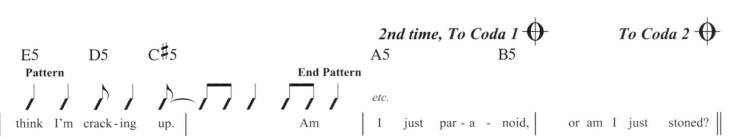

     | think   I'm   crack - ing   up.   Am   *etc.* | I   just   par - a - noid, | or   am   I   just   stoned? ||

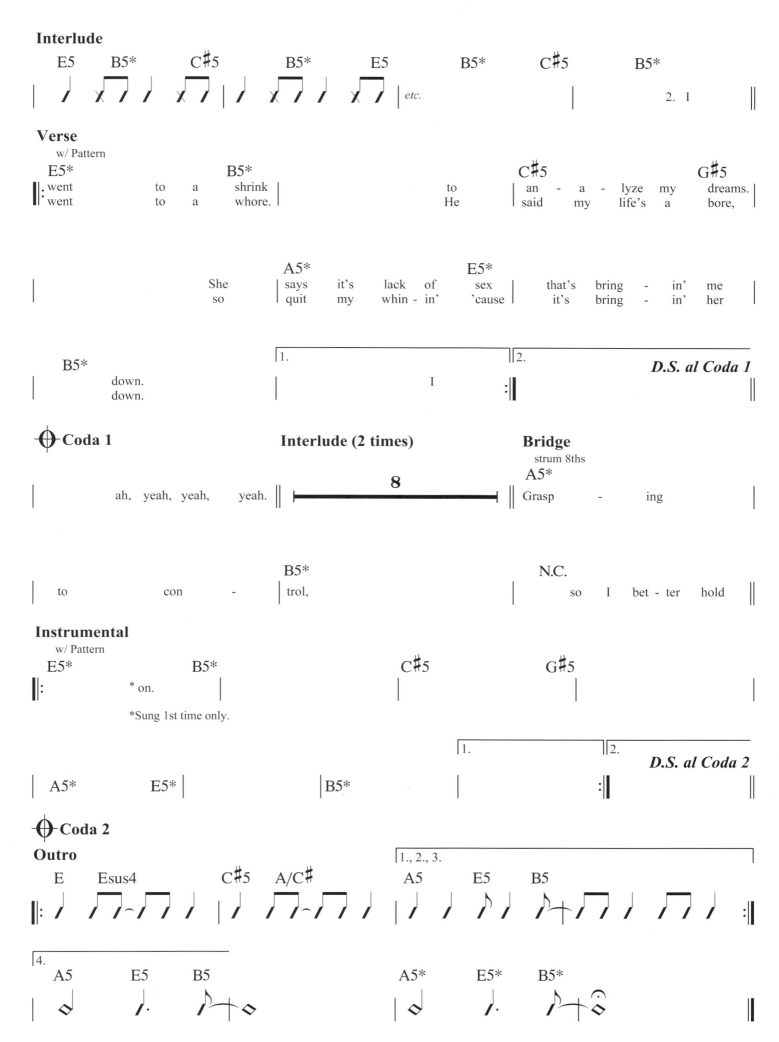

Beat It

Words and Music by Michael Jackson

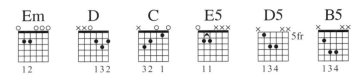

Tune down 1/2 step:
(low to high) Eb-Ab-Db-Gb-Bb-Eb

Key of Em

Intro

Moderately fast

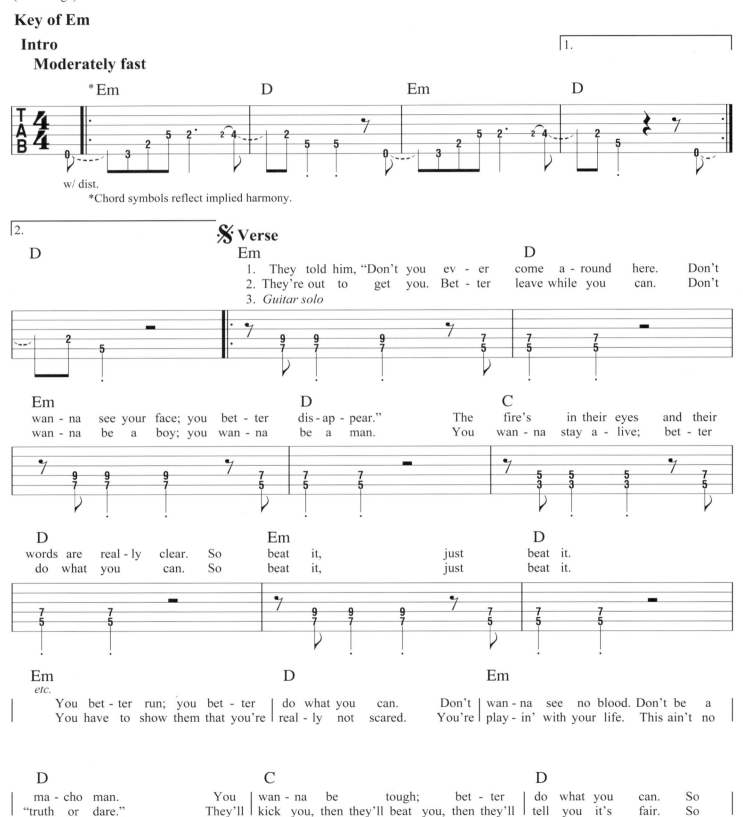

w/ dist.

*Chord symbols reflect implied harmony.

Verse

1. They told him, "Don't you ev - er come a - round here. Don't
2. They're out to get you. Bet - ter leave while you can. Don't
3. *Guitar solo*

wan - na see your face; you bet - ter dis - ap - pear." The fire's in their eyes and their
wan - na be a boy; you wan - na be a man. You wan - na stay a - live; bet - ter

words are real - ly clear. So beat it, just beat it.
do what you can. So beat it, just beat it.

etc.

You bet - ter run; you bet - ter do what you can. Don't wan - na see no blood. Don't be a
You have to show them that you're real - ly not scared. You're play - in' with your life. This ain't no

ma - cho man. You wan - na be tough; bet - ter do what you can. So
"truth or dare." They'll kick you, then they'll beat you, then they'll tell you it's fair. So

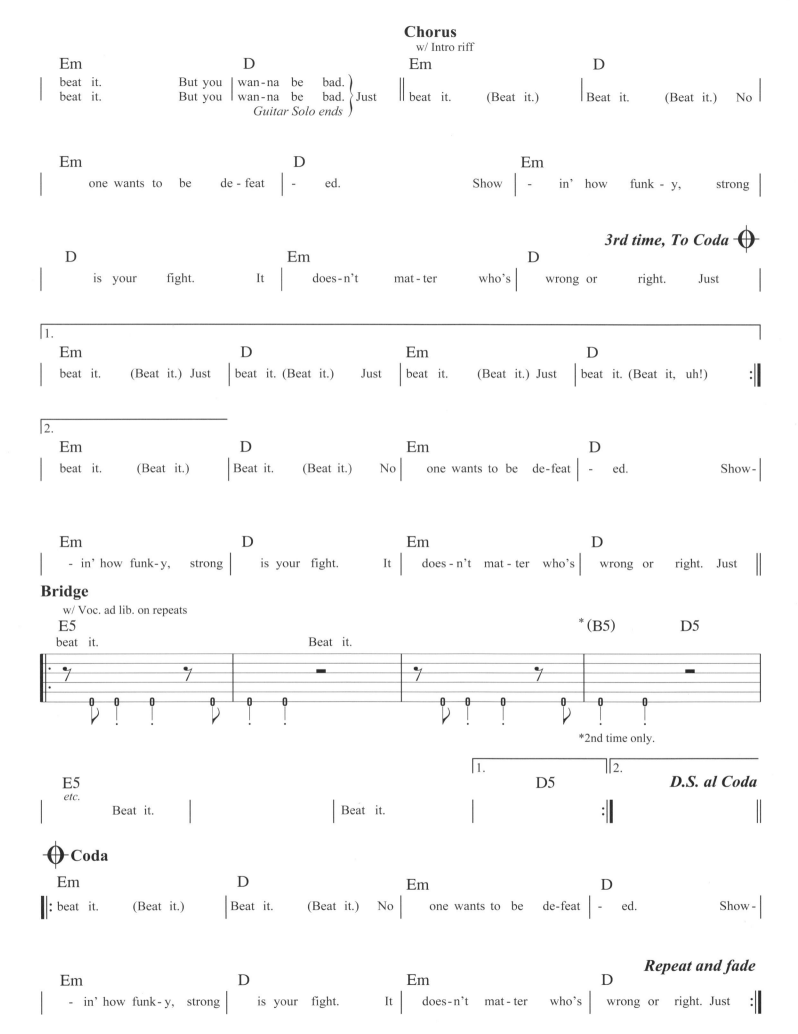

Boom Boom

Words and Music by John Lee Hooker

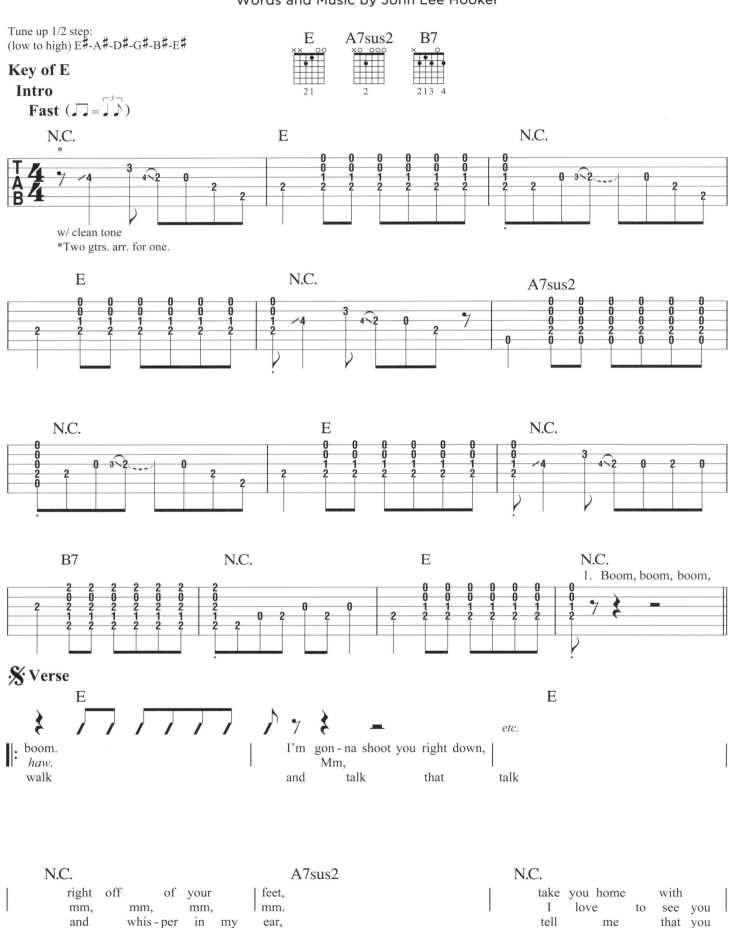

Tune up 1/2 step:
(low to high) E#-A#-D#-G#-B#-E#

Key of E

Intro

Fast (♪♪ = ♪♪)

w/ clean tone
*Two gtrs. arr. for one.

1. Boom, boom, boom,

Verse

boom.
haw.
walk

I'm gon-na shoot you right down,
Mm,
and talk that talk

right off of your feet,
mm, mm, mm,
and whis-per in my ear,

take you home with
I love to see you
tell me that you

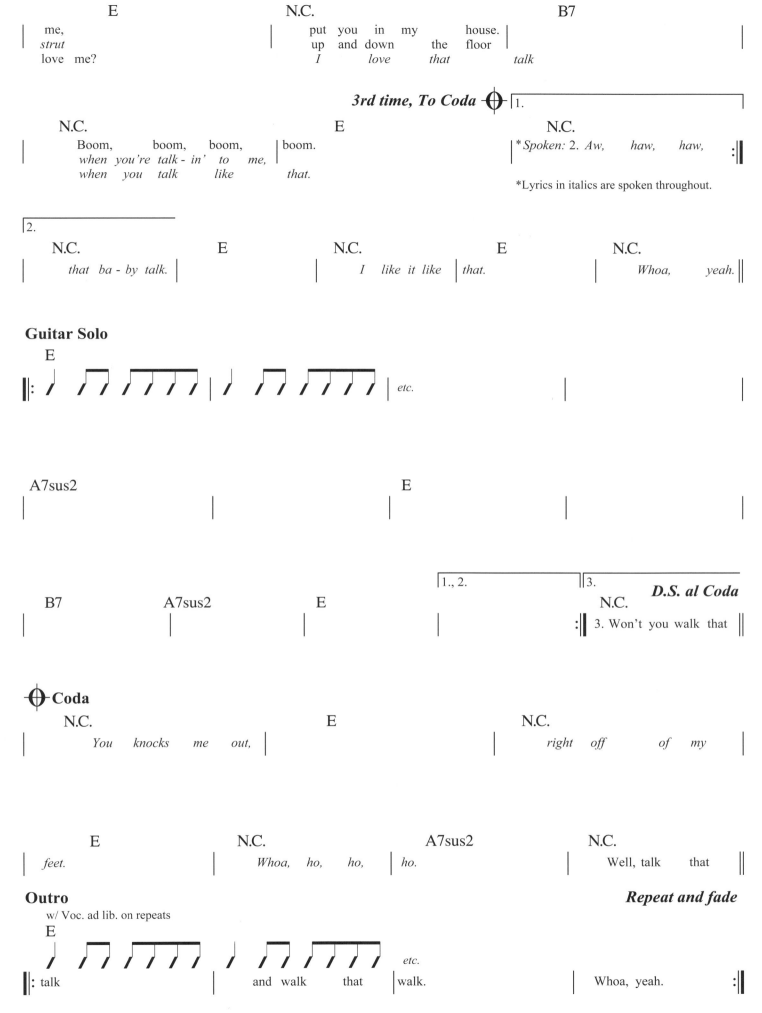

Born to Be Wild

Words and Music by Mars Bonfire

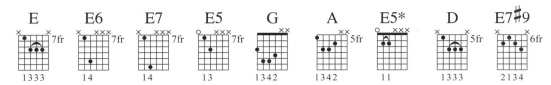

Key of E

Intro

Moderately fast

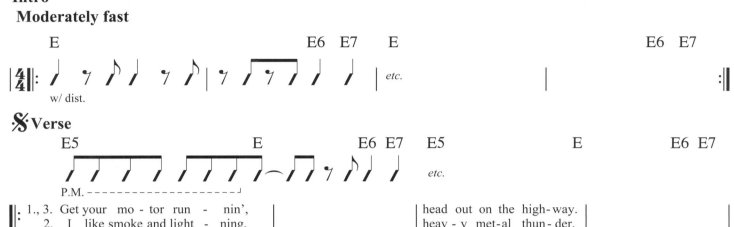

Verse

P.M.

1., 3. Get your mo-tor run-nin',   head out on the high-way.
2. I like smoke and light-ning,   heav-y met-al thun-der,

Look-in' for ad-ven-ture   and what-ev-er comes our way.
rac-in' with the wind,   and the feel in' that I'm un-der.

Pre-Chorus

Yeah, dar-lin', go make it hap-pen,   take the world in a love em-brace.

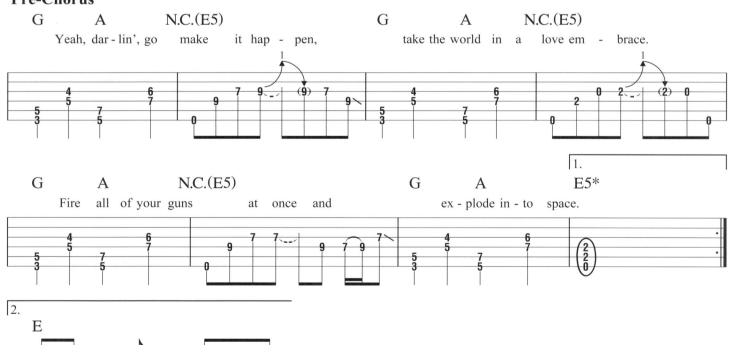

Fire all of your guns at once and   ex-plode in-to space.

Like a true na-ture's child   we were

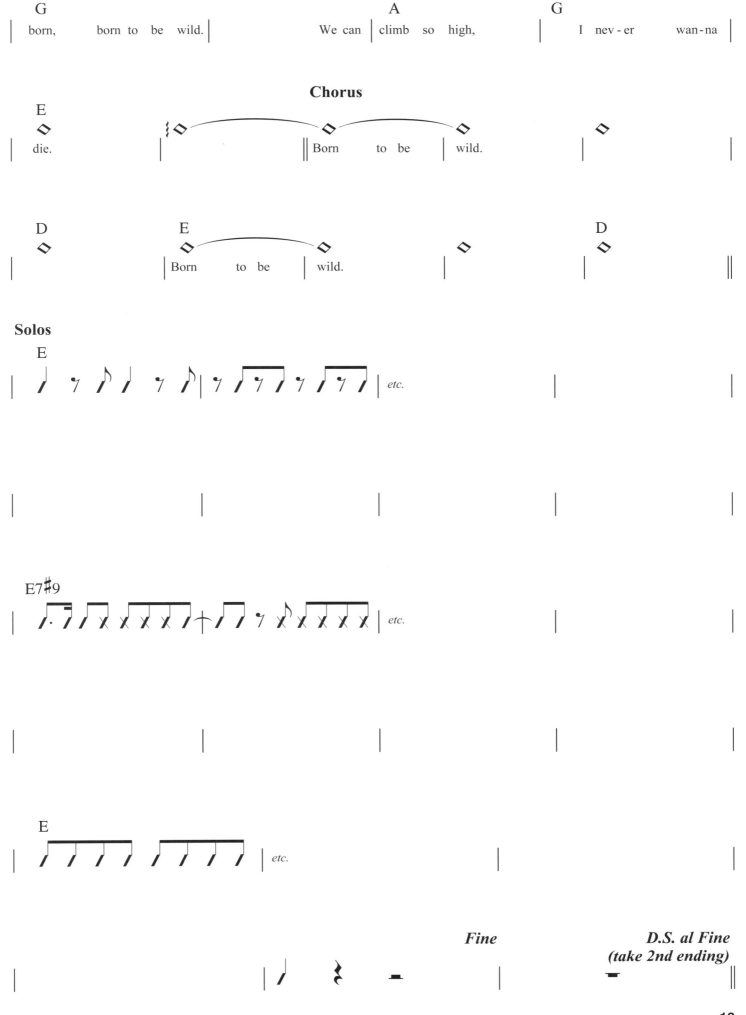

Breaking the Law

Words and Music by Glenn Tipton, Rob Halford and K.K. Downing

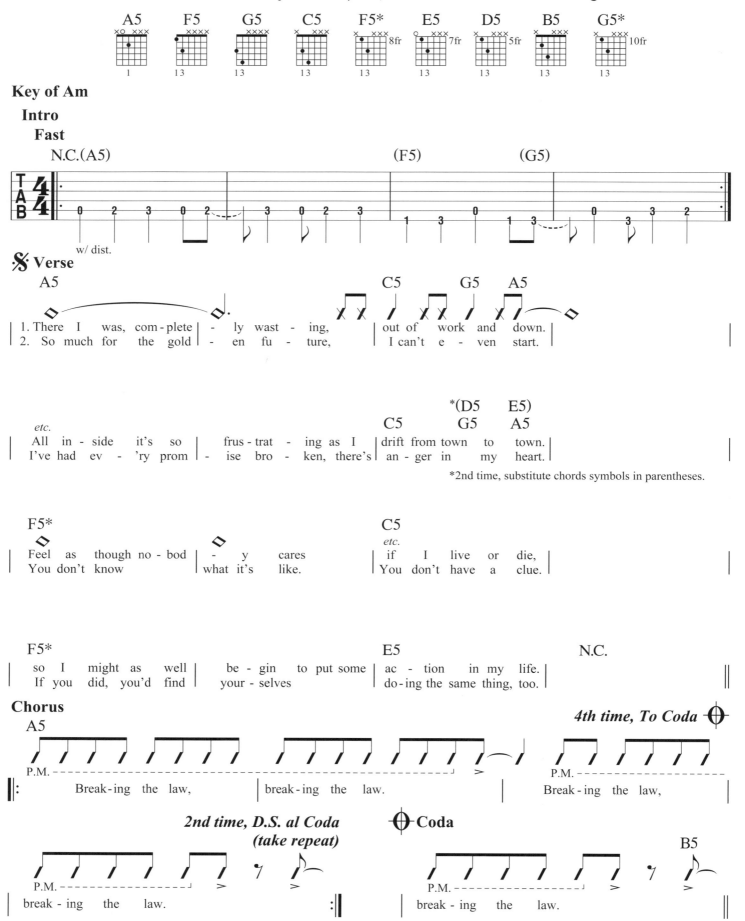

Bridge

A5   B5   A5   *Play 3 times*

etc.

D5   F5*   C5   D5   F5*   G5*

You   don't   know what it's   like.   *etc.*

D5   F5   C5   D5   F5   G5*

Interlude

w/ Intro riff

‖: N.C.(A5)   (F5)   (G5)   :‖

A5   F5   G5

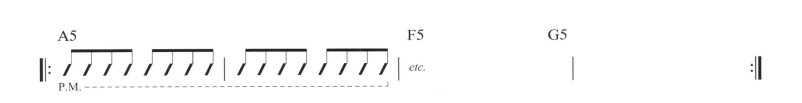

P.M. –   *etc.*

Outro-Chorus

A5   F5   G5

‖:   Break-ing the law,   break-ing the law.   Break-ing the law,

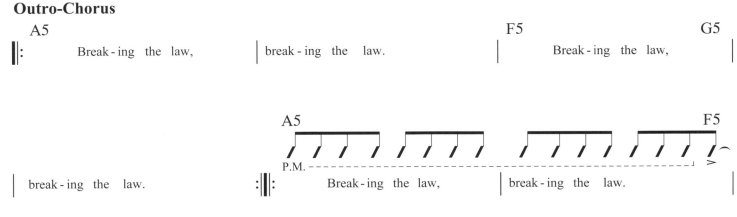

                                   A5   F5

P.M. – >

break-ing the law.   :‖:   Break-ing the law,   break-ing the law.

1.   **2.**

          G5   A5   A5

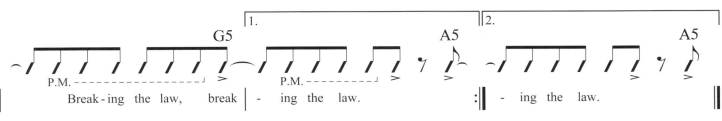

P.M. – – – – – – – – – – – – >   P.M. – – – – – – >

Break-ing the law, break - ing the law.   :‖ - ing the law.

Brown Eyed Girl

Words and Music by Van Morrison

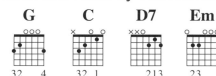

Key of G

Intro

Moderately fast

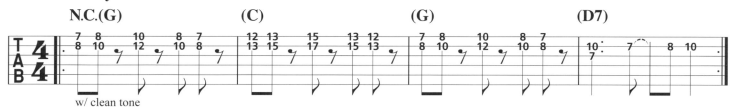

w/ clean tone

Verse

1. Hey, where did we | go? | Days when the rains | came, |
2., 3. *See additional lyrics*

down in the | hol - low, | play - in' a new | game, |

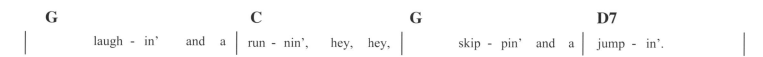

laugh - in' and a | run - nin', hey, hey, | skip - pin' and a | jump - in'. |

In the mist - y morn | - in' fog with | our, our | hearts a thump - in' and you, |

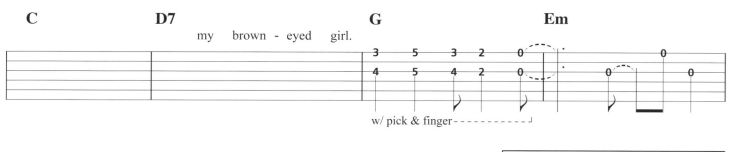

my brown - eyed girl.

w/ pick & finger

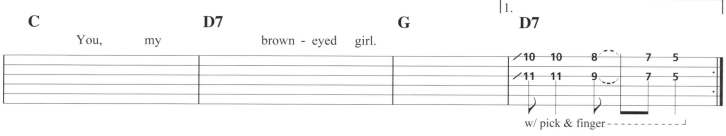

You, my brown - eyed girl.

w/ pick & finger

To Coda ⊕

D7

	Do you re-mem-	ber when		we used to sing:

Chorus

G　　　　　　**C**　　　　　　**G**　　　**D7**

Sha, la, la, la, | la, la, la, la, | la, la, la, te da. |

G　　　　　　**C**　　　　　　**G**　　　**D7**

Sha, la, la, la, | la, la, la, la, | la, la, la, te da. | La, te da.

G　　　　　　　　　　　　　　　　　　　**N.C.**

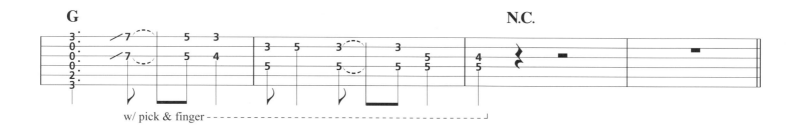

w/ pick & finger -

D.S. al Coda

Bass Solo
N.C.

⊕ **Coda**

Repeat and fade

Outro-Chorus

G　　　　　　**C**　　　　　　**G**　　　**D7**

‖: Sha, la, la, la, | la, la, la, la, | la, la, la, te da. | :‖

Additional Lyrics

2. Whatever happened
   To Tuesday and so slow,
   Going down the old mine
   With a transistor radio?
   Standing in the sunlight laughing,
   Hiding behind a rainbow's wall,
   Slipping and a-sliding
   All along the waterfall
   With you, my brown eyed girl.
   You, my brown eyed girl.
   Do you remember when we used to sing;

3. So hard to find my way,
   Now that I'm all on my own.
   I saw you just the other day,
   My, how you have grown.
   Cast my memory back there, Lord,
   Sometimes I'm overcome thinkin' 'bout it.
   Making love in the green grass
   Behind the stadium
   With you, my brown eyed girl,
   You, my brown eyed girl.
   Do you remember when we used to sing;

Californication

Words and Music by Anthony Kiedis, Flea, John Frusciante and Chad Smith

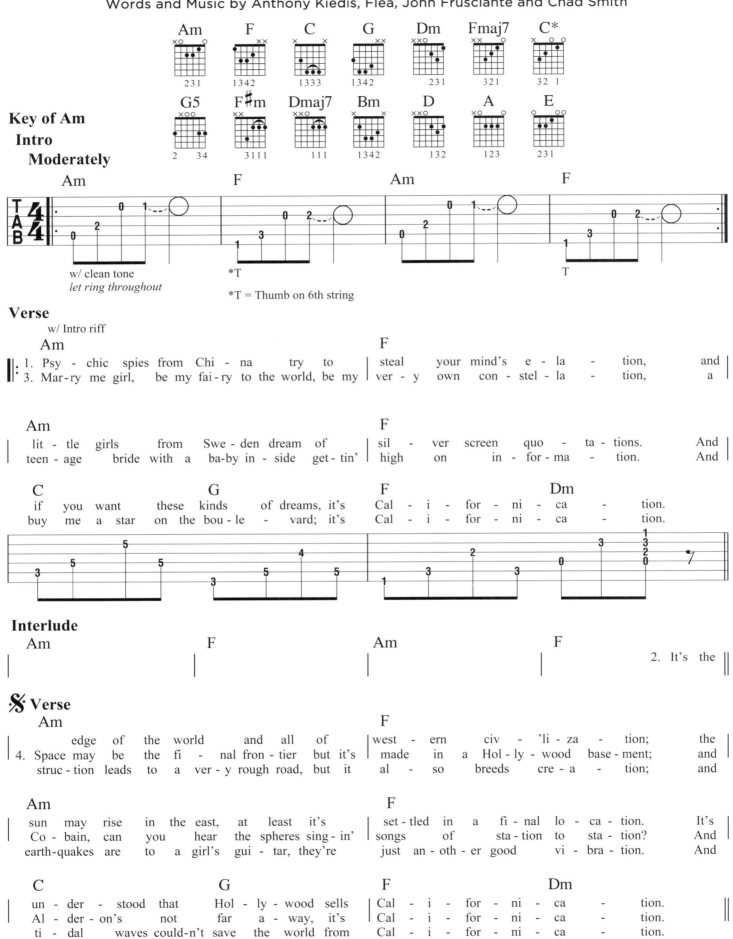

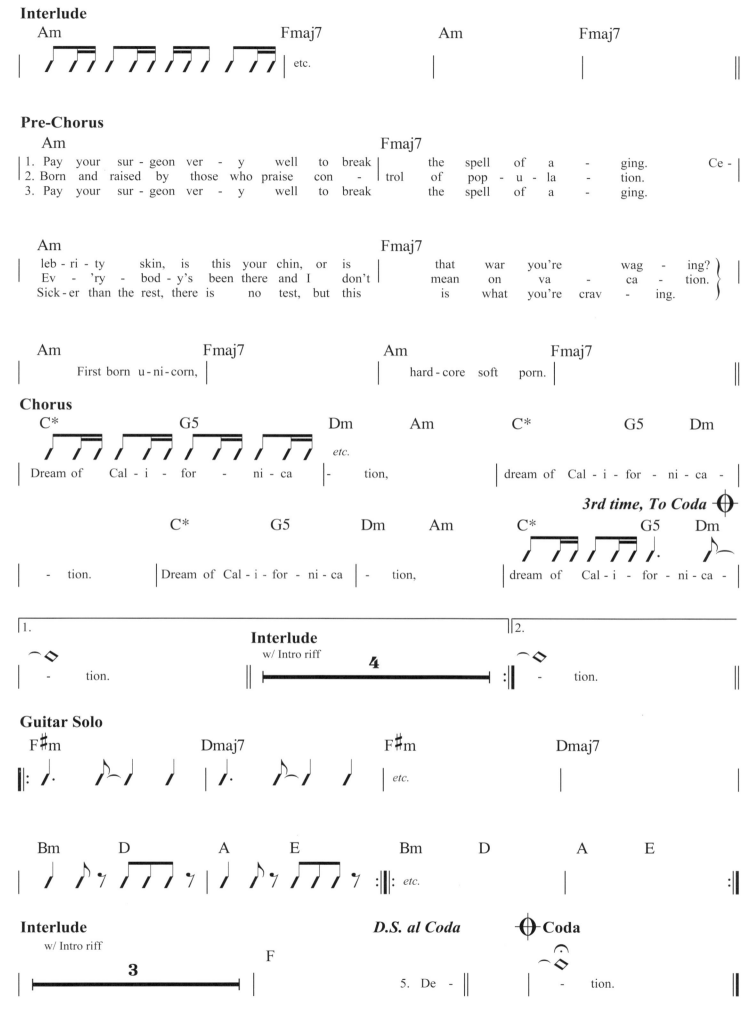

Cocaine

Words and Music by J.J. Cale

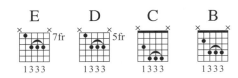

Key of E

Intro
Moderately

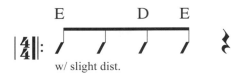

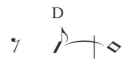

w/ slight dist.

etc.

1.

2.

1. If you

% Verse

|| wan - na hang out, you've got - ta take her out, co - caine. |
got bad news, you wan - na kick the blues, co - caine. |
thing is done and ya wan - na ride on, co - caine. |

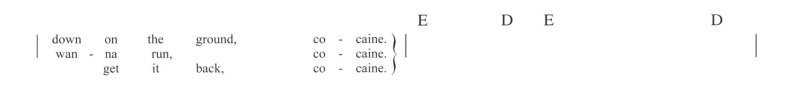

If you | wan - na get down,
When your | day is done an' you |
Don't for - get this fact, can't |

| down on the ground, co - caine. }
| wan - na run, co - caine. }
get it back, co - caine. }

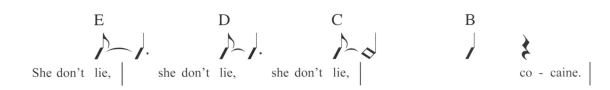

| She don't lie, she don't lie, she don't lie, co - caine. |

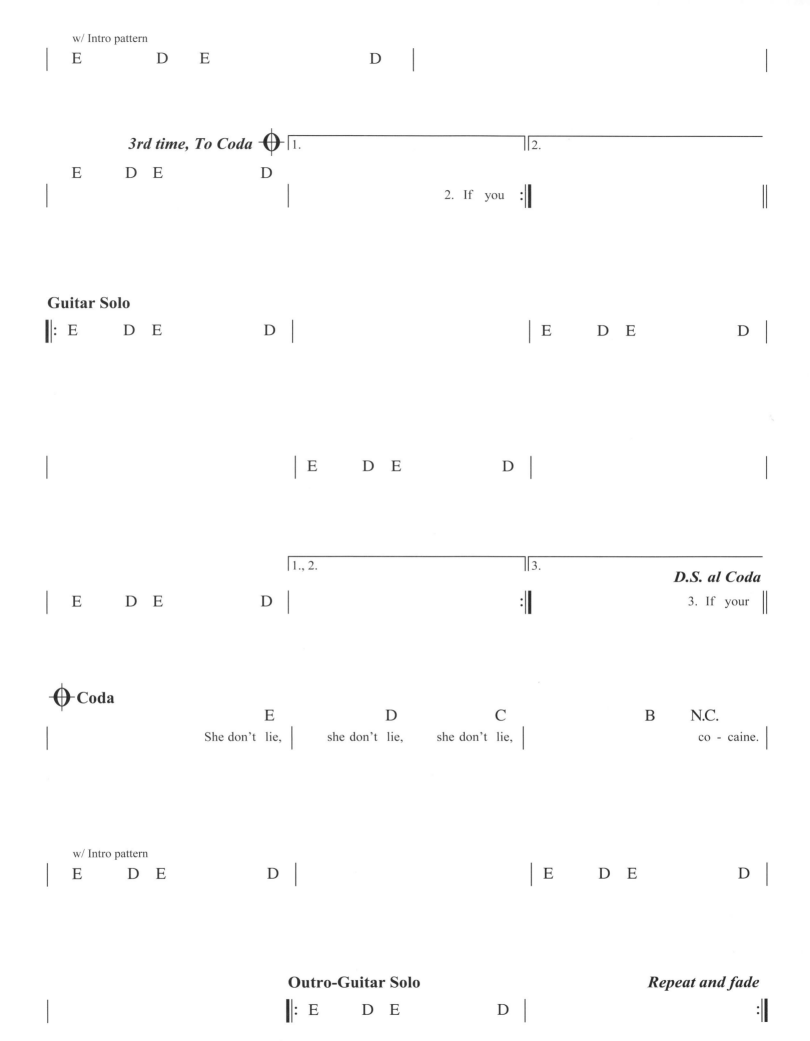

Come as You Are

Words and Music by Kurt Cobain

Tune down 1 step:
(low to high) D-G-C-F-A-D

Key of F#m

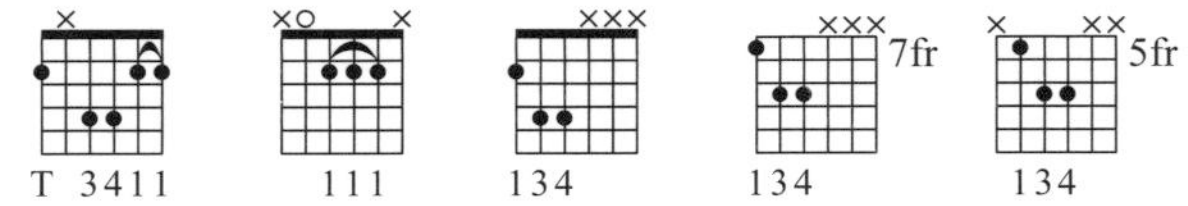

Intro

Moderately

N.C.

Play 4 times

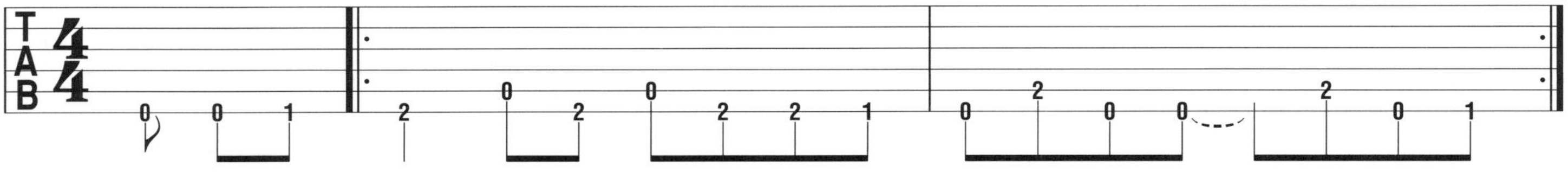

w/ clean tone & chorus

%Verse

N.C.

etc.

1. Come as you are, as you were, as I want you to be;
3. *Guitar Solo*

as a friend, as a friend, as an old

en - e - my. 2. Come Take your time, hur - ry up,
Take doused in mud, soaked in bleach,

the choice is yours, don't be late. Take a rest
as I want you to be; as a trend,

as a friend, as an old mem - o - ry,
as a friend, as an old mem - o - ry,
Guitar Solo ends Mem - o - ry,

Pre-Chorus

F#sus4   A   F#sus4

etc.

ah, mem - o - ry, ah,

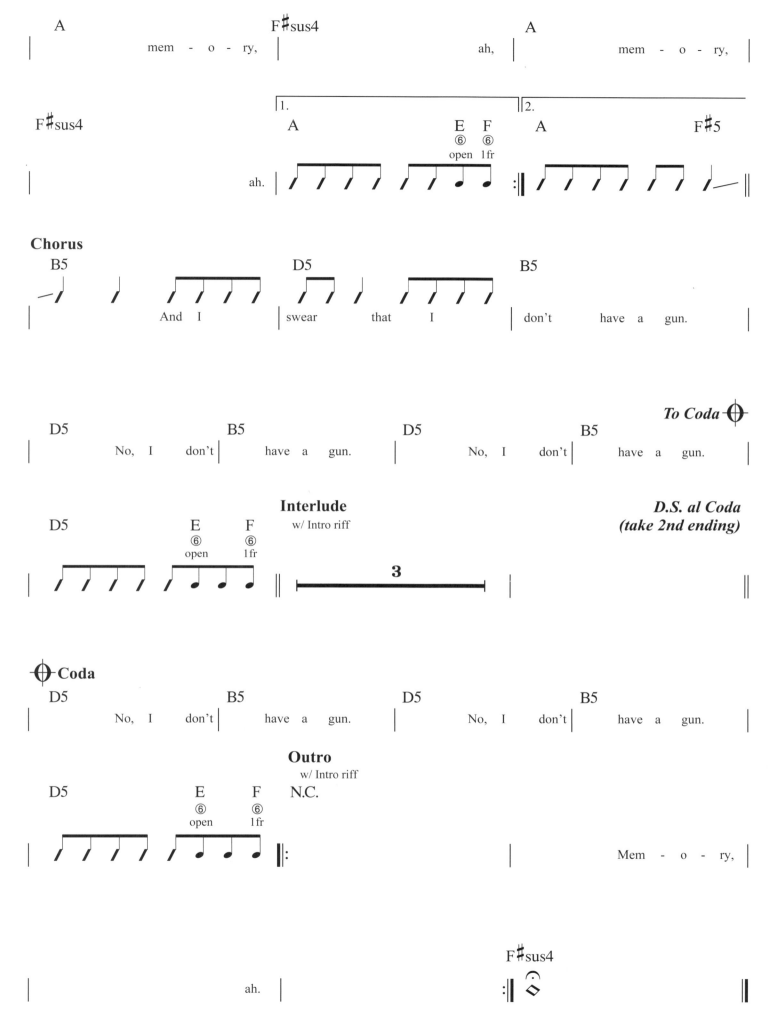

Communication Breakdown

Words and Music by Jimmy Page, John Paul Jones and John Bonham

E5   D   A   A5   A7   B5   B7   E

Key of E

Intro

Fast

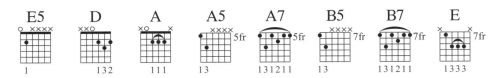

Verse

	E5		D	A	D	E5
1. Hey,		girl,		stop		what you're do - in'.
2. Hey,		girl,		I got		some - thing I think you ought

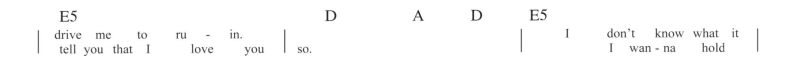

D	A	D	E5		D	A	D
to know.		Hey,	Hey,	girl,	babe,	I wan - na

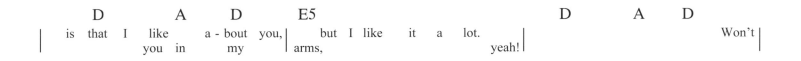

E5		D	A	D	E5	
drive me to ru - in.			I don't know what it
tell you that I love you	so.		I wan - na hold

D	A	D	E5		D	A	D
is that I like a - bout you,	but I like it a lot.			Won't
you in my	arms,	yeah!		

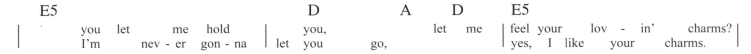

E5		D	A	D	E5
you let me hold you,	let me	feel your lov - in' charms?
I'm nev - er gon - na	let you go,	yes, I like your charms.

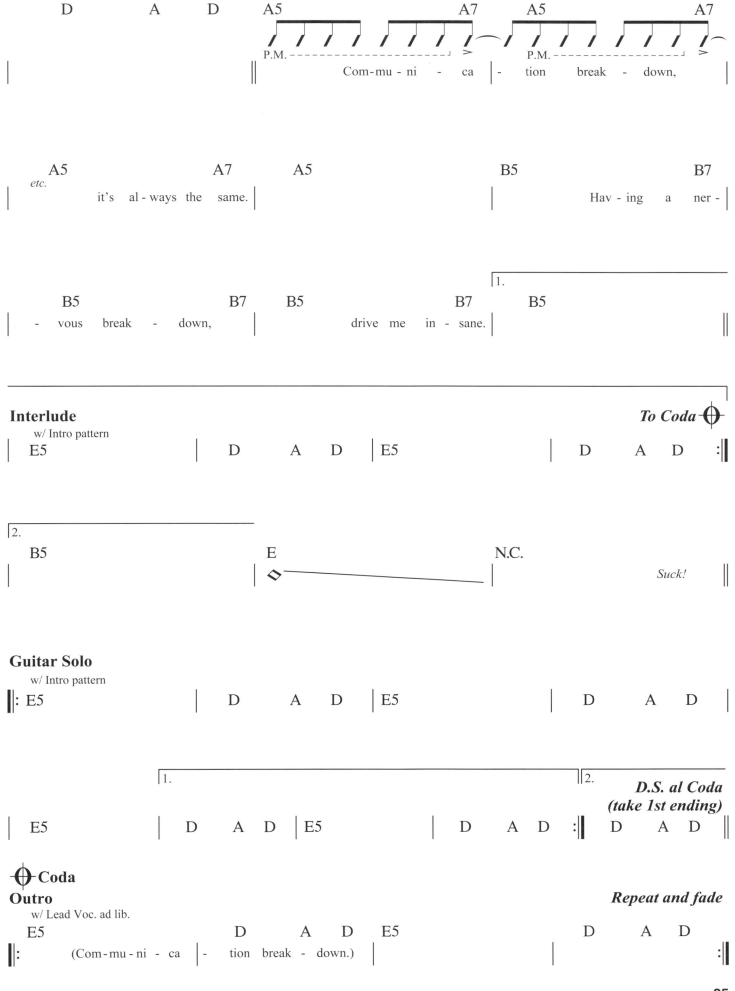

Creep

**Words and Music by Albert Hammond, Mike Hazlewood, Thomas Yorke,
Jonathan Greenwood, Colin Greenwood, Edward O'Brien and Philip Selway**

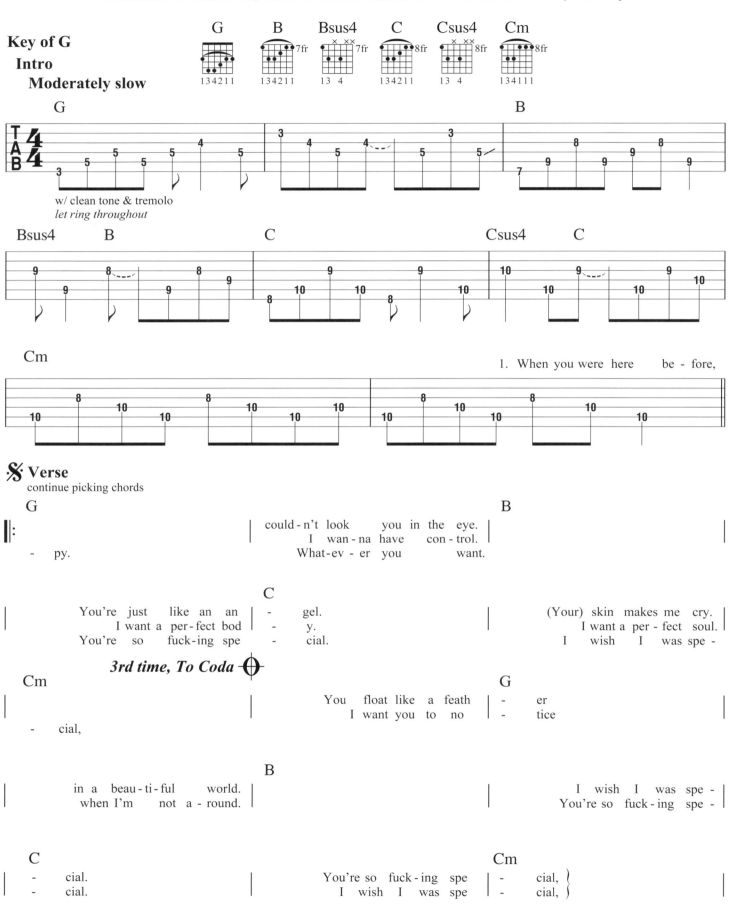

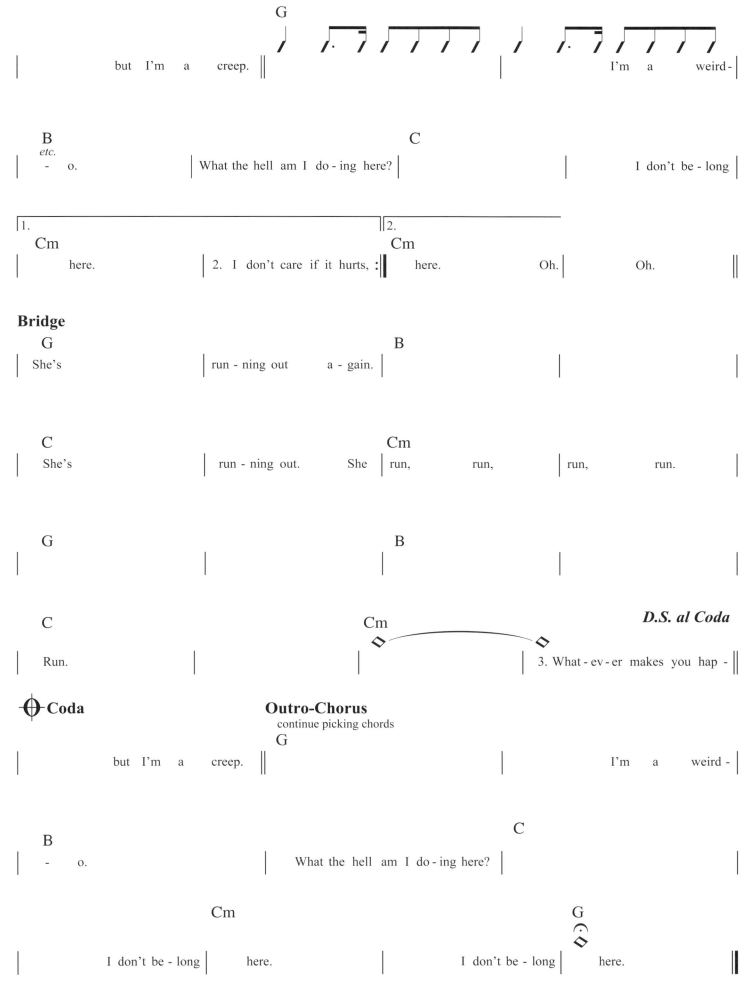

Day Tripper

Words and Music by John Lennon and Paul McCartney

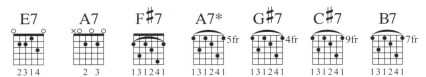

Key of E

Intro

Moderately fast

N.C.(E7)

w/ clean tone

etc.
‖: E7   *Play 3 times*

Verse

w/ Intro riff

E7

```
1. Got     a     good   rea  -  son                                    for
2. She's   a     big    teas  -  er.
3. Tried   to    please her,
```

```
tak - ing   the   eas  -  y    way   out.
She   took  me    half       the   way   there.
she   on - ly  played     one - night  stands.
```

A7

```
Got     a     good   rea  -  son                                      for
She's   a     big    teas  -  er.
Tried   to    please her,
```

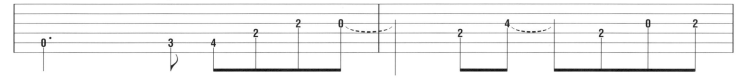

E7

```
tak - ing   the   eas  -  y    way   out,        now.  ⎫
She   took  me    half       the   way   there,   now.  ⎬         She   was   a
she   on - ly  played     one - night  stands,   now.  ⎭
```

Chorus

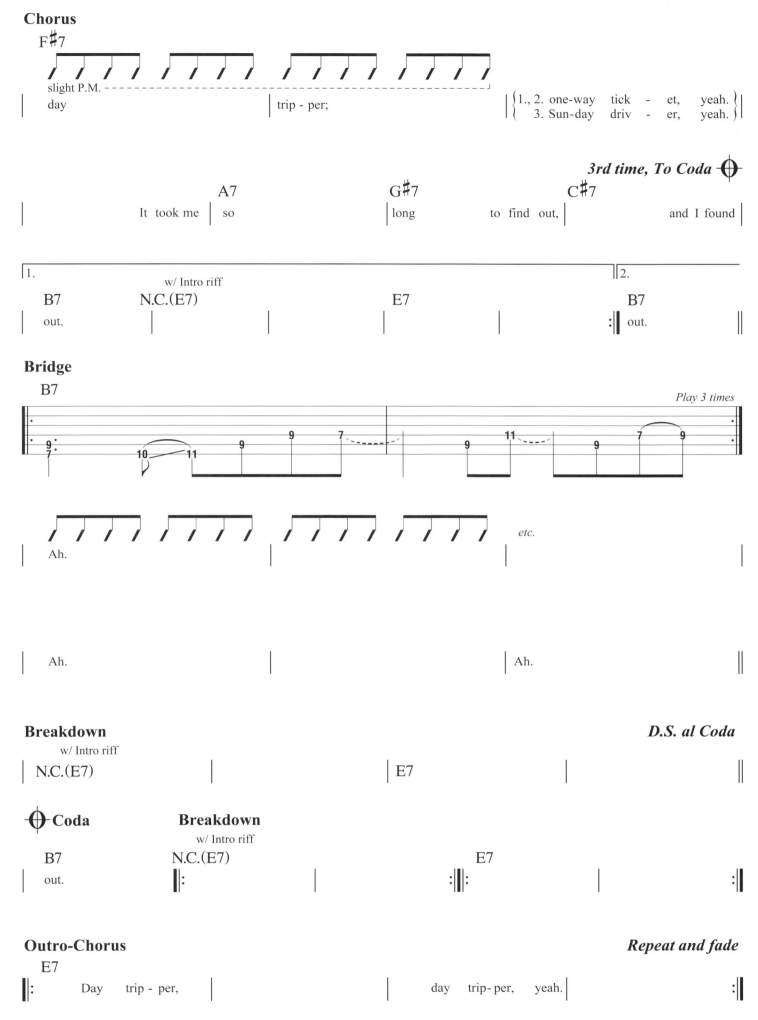

F#7

slight P.M. -

day | trip - per; | {1., 2. one-way tick - et, yeah. } | {3. Sun-day driv - er, yeah. }

3rd time, To Coda ⊕

A7   G#7   C#7

It took me | so   long   to find out, | and I found |

1.

w/ Intro riff

B7   N.C.(E7)   E7   2.   B7

out. | | | | :‖ out. ‖

Bridge

B7

Play 3 times

Ah.   *etc.*

Ah. | | Ah. ‖

Breakdown   *D.S. al Coda*

w/ Intro riff

N.C.(E7) | | E7 | ‖

⊕ **Coda**   **Breakdown**

w/ Intro riff

B7   N.C.(E7)   E7

out. | ‖: | | :‖‖: | :‖

Outro-Chorus   *Repeat and fade*

E7

‖: Day trip - per, | day trip- per, yeah. | :‖

29

Detroit Rock City

Words and Music by Paul Stanley and Bob Ezrin

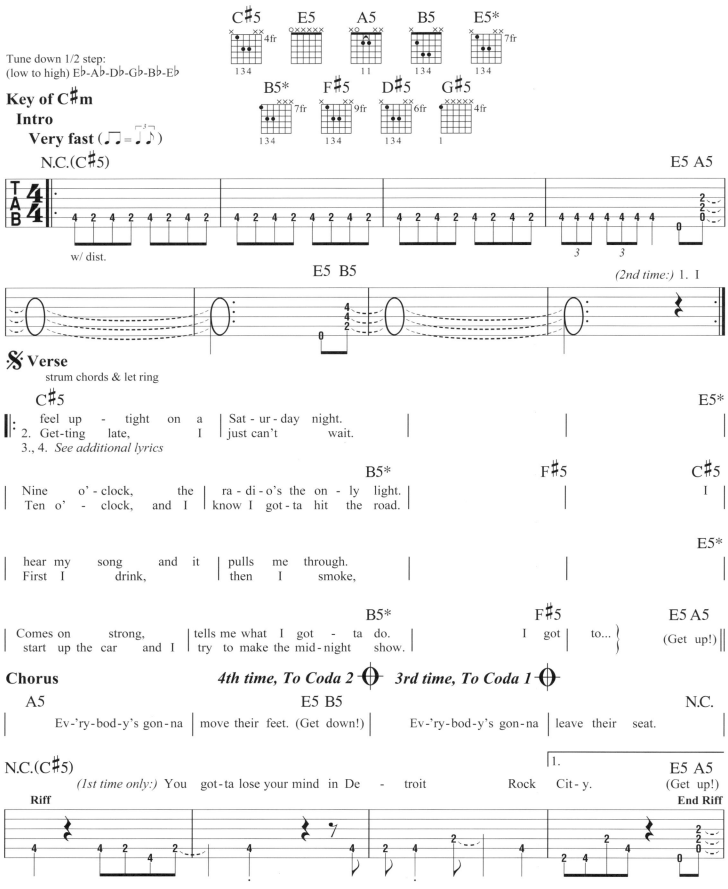

Tune down 1/2 step:
(low to high) Eb-Ab-Db-Gb-Bb-Eb

Key of C#m
Intro
Very fast (♩♩ = ♩♪)

w/ dist.

(2nd time:) 1. I

% Verse
strum chords & let ring

feel up - tight on a | Sat - ur - day night.
2. Get - ting late, I | just can't wait.
3., 4. See additional lyrics

Nine o' - clock, the | ra - di - o's the on - ly light. | I
Ten o' - clock, and I | know I got - ta hit the road.

hear my song and it | pulls me through.
First I drink, then I smoke,

Comes on strong, | tells me what I got - ta do. | I got | to... } (Get up!)
start up the car and I | try to make the mid - night show.

Chorus
4th time, To Coda 2 ⊕ *3rd time, To Coda 1* ⊕

Ev - 'ry - bod - y's gon - na | move their feet. (Get down!) | Ev - 'ry - bod - y's gon - na | leave their seat.

N.C.(C#5)
(1st time only:) You got - ta lose your mind in De - troit Rock Cit - y. (Get up!)

Riff   **End Riff**

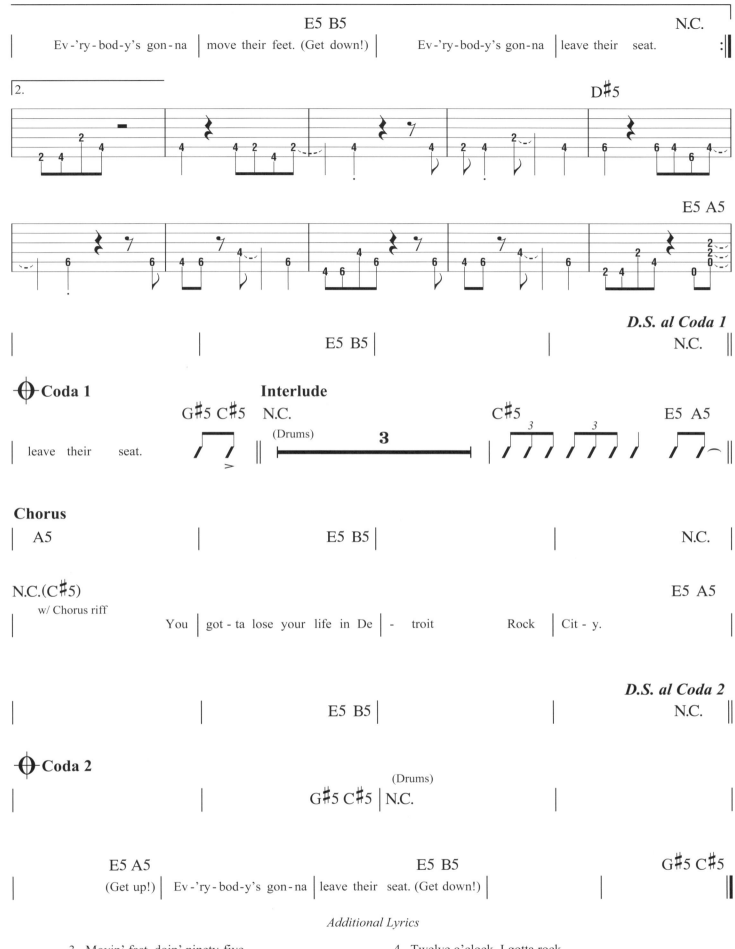

E5 B5   **N.C.**

Ev-'ry-bod-y's gon-na | move their feet. (Get down!)   Ev-'ry-bod-y's gon-na | leave their   seat.

D.S. al Coda 1

Coda 1   **Interlude**

| leave   their   seat.

Chorus

A5   **E5 B5**   **N.C.**

N.C.(C#5)   **E5 A5**
w/ Chorus riff

You | got-ta lose your life in De | - troit   Rock | Cit-y.

D.S. al Coda 2

E5 B5 | **N.C.**

Coda 2
(Drums)
G#5 C#5 | N.C.

E5 A5   **E5 B5**   **G#5 C#5**
(Get up!) | Ev-'ry-bod-y's gon-na | leave their   seat. (Get down!)

Additional Lyrics

3. Movin' fast, doin' ninety-five.
   Hit top speed, but I'm still movin' much too slow.
   I feel so good, I'm so alive.
   Hear my song playin' on the radio. It goes...

4. Twelve o'clock, I gotta rock.
   There's a truck ahead, lights starin' at my eyes.
   Oh, my God, no time to turn.
   I got to laugh 'cause I know I'm gonna die. Why?

Dirty Deeds Done Dirt Cheap

Words and Music by Angus Young, Malcolm Young and Bon Scott

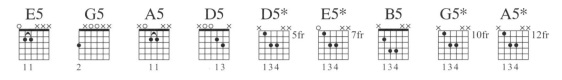

E5 G5 A5 D5 D5* E5* B5 G5* A5*

Key of E

Intro

Moderately fast

1., 2., 3.   4.

E5 G5 E5 A5 E5 D5 E5 E5 D5*

w/ dist.

$\frac{4}{4}$

1. If you're

%‌ Verse

E5*

hav-in' trou-ble with the	high school head,		he's giv-in' you the blues.
You got	prob-lems in your	life of love,	you got a bro-ken heart.
got a la-dy and you	want her gone,	but you ain't got the guts.

D5* E5*

etc.

You wan-na grad-u-ate but	not in his bed,
He's dou-ble deal-in' with your	best friend,
She keeps nag-ging at you night and	day,

D5* E5*

here's what you've got-ta do:	Pick up the phone, I'm
that's when the tear-drops start,	fel-la.	Pick up the phone, I'm
e-nough to drive you nuts.	Pick up the phone, leave

D5*

al-ways home,	call me an-y-time.	Just ring:
here a-lone,	I'll make a so-cial call.
her a-lone,	it's time you made a stand.

E5* D5* E5* D5* E5* D5*

three-six-two-four	-three-six. Hey,	I lead a life of crime.
Come right in, for	-get a-bout him.	We'll have our-selves a ball.
For a fee, I'm	hap-py to be	your back door man.

Chorus

E5* A5 G5 A5

| Dirt-y deeds | done dirt cheap. |

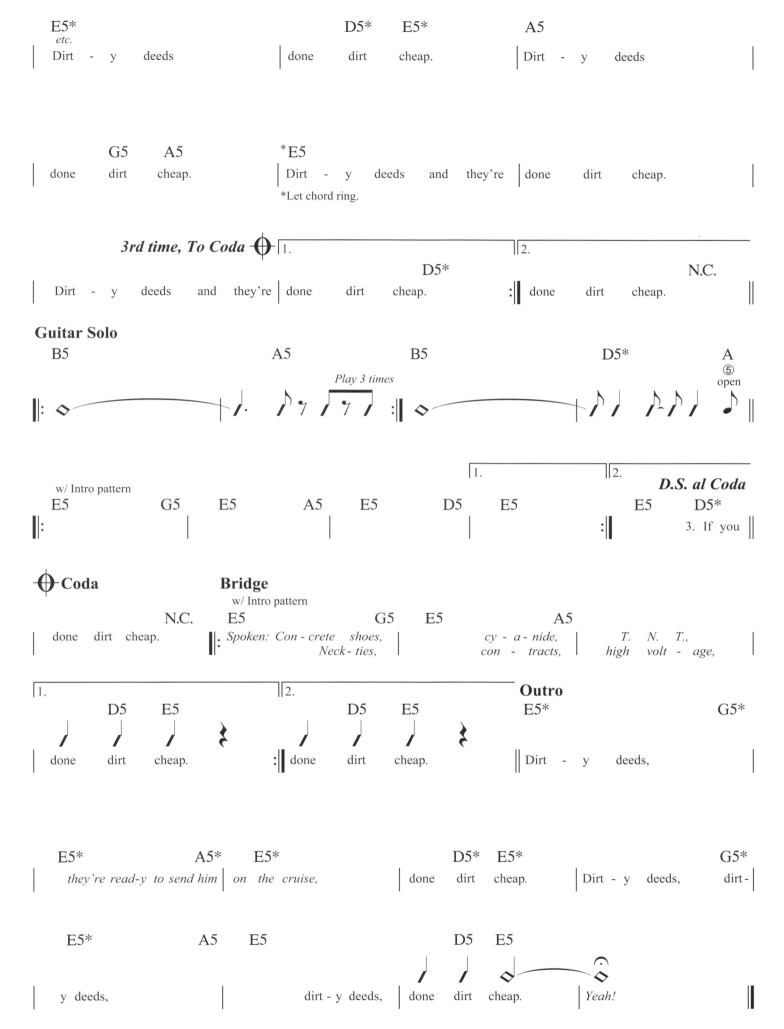

Everybody Hurts

Words and Music by William Berry, Peter Buck, Michael Mills and Michael Stipe

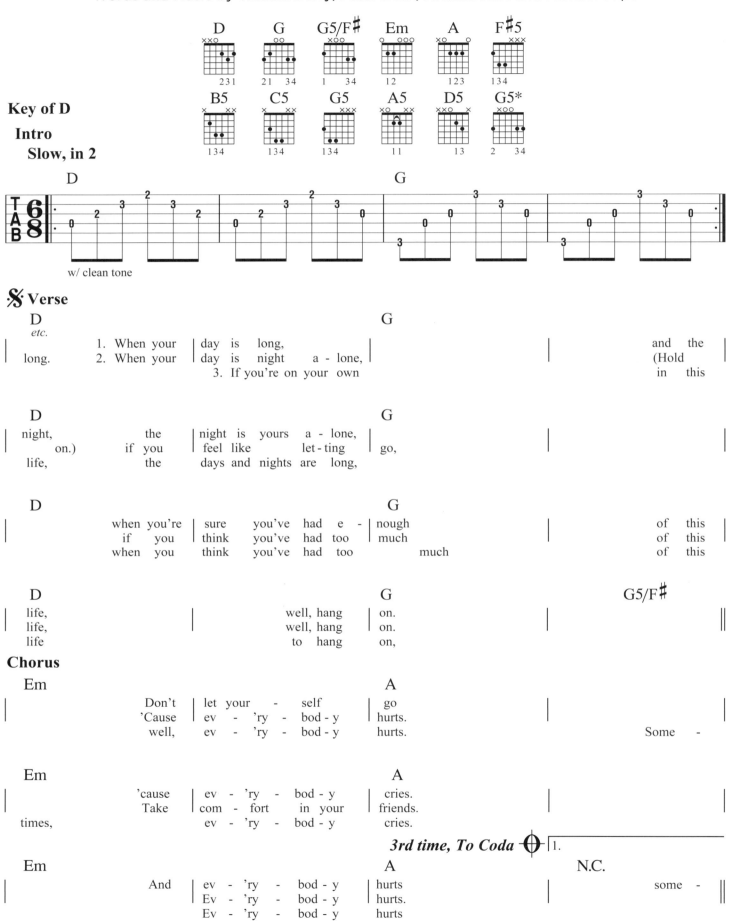

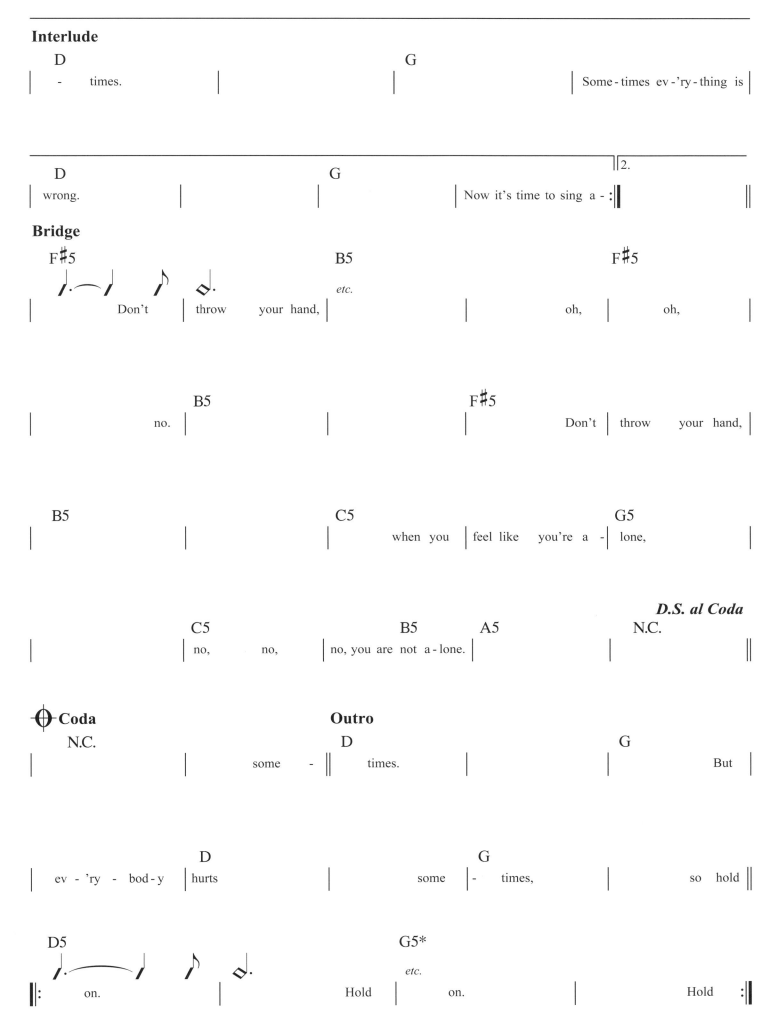

Interlude

D   G

| -   times. | | | Some - times ev - 'ry - thing is |

D   G   2.

| wrong. | | | Now it's time to sing a - : ‖

Bridge

F♯5   B5   F♯5

| Don't | throw   your hand, | *etc.* | oh, | oh, | |

          B5   F♯5

| no. | | | Don't | throw   your hand, |

B5   C5   G5

| | | when you | feel like   you're a - | lone, | |

                                             D.S. al Coda

         C5   B5   A5   N.C.

| | no,   no, | no, you are not a - lone. | | ‖

⊕ **Coda**   **Outro**

   N.C.   D   G

| | some - ‖ times. | | But |

                 D   G

| ev - 'ry - bod - y | hurts | | some | - times, | | so hold ‖

D5   G5*

‖:   on. | | Hold   *etc.* | on. | | Hold :‖

Hallelujah

Words and Music by Leonard Cohen

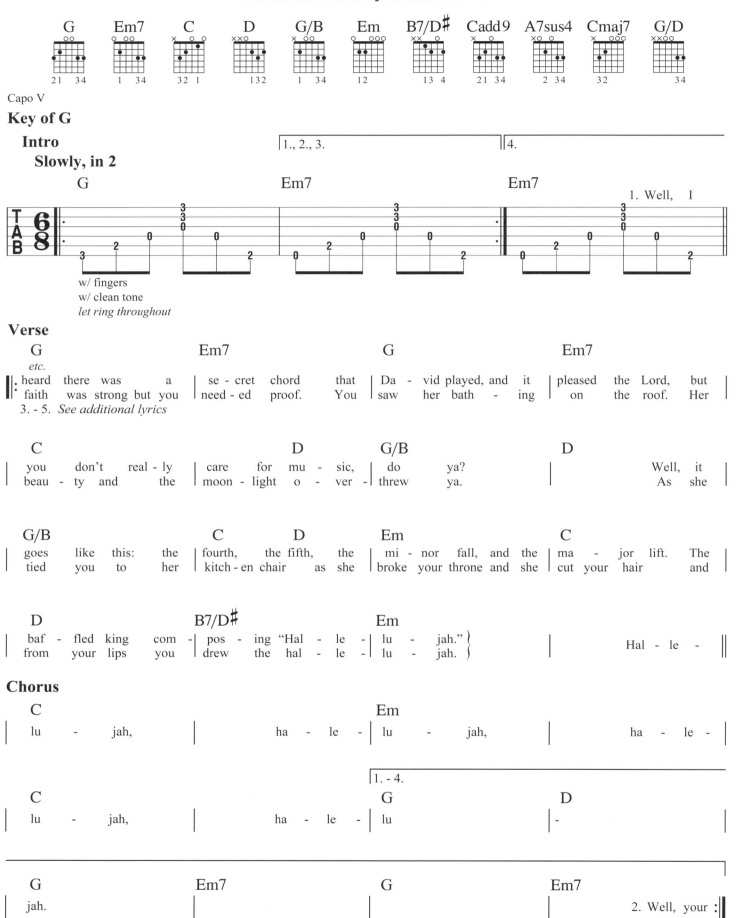

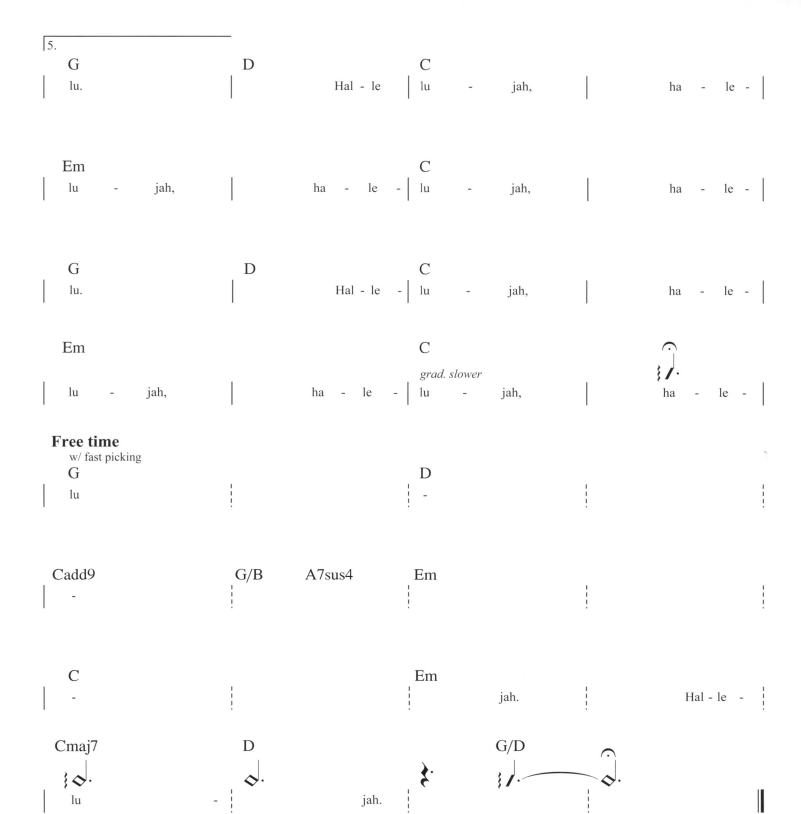

Additional Lyrics

3. Well, baby, I've been here before,
   I've seen this room and I've walked this floor,
   You know, I used to live alone before I knew ya.
   And I've seen your flag on the marble arch,
   And love is not a vict'ry march,
   It's a cold and it's a broken hallelujah.

4. Well, there was a time when you let me know
   What's really going on below.
   But now you never show that to me, do ya?
   But remember when I moved in you
   And the holy dove was moving too,
   And ev'ry breath we drew was hallelujah.

5. Maybe there is a God above,
   But all I've ever learned from love
   Was how to shoot somebody who outdrew ya.
   And it's not a cry that you hear at night,
   It's not somebody who's seen the light,
   It's a cold and it's a broken hallelujah.

Here Without You

Words and Music by Matt Roberts, Brad Arnold, Christopher Henderson and Robert Harrell

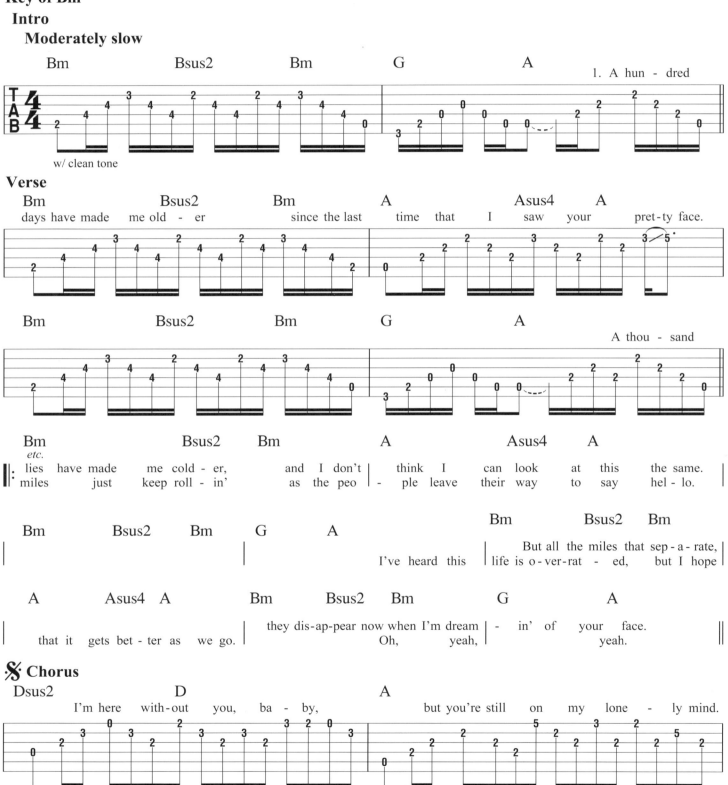

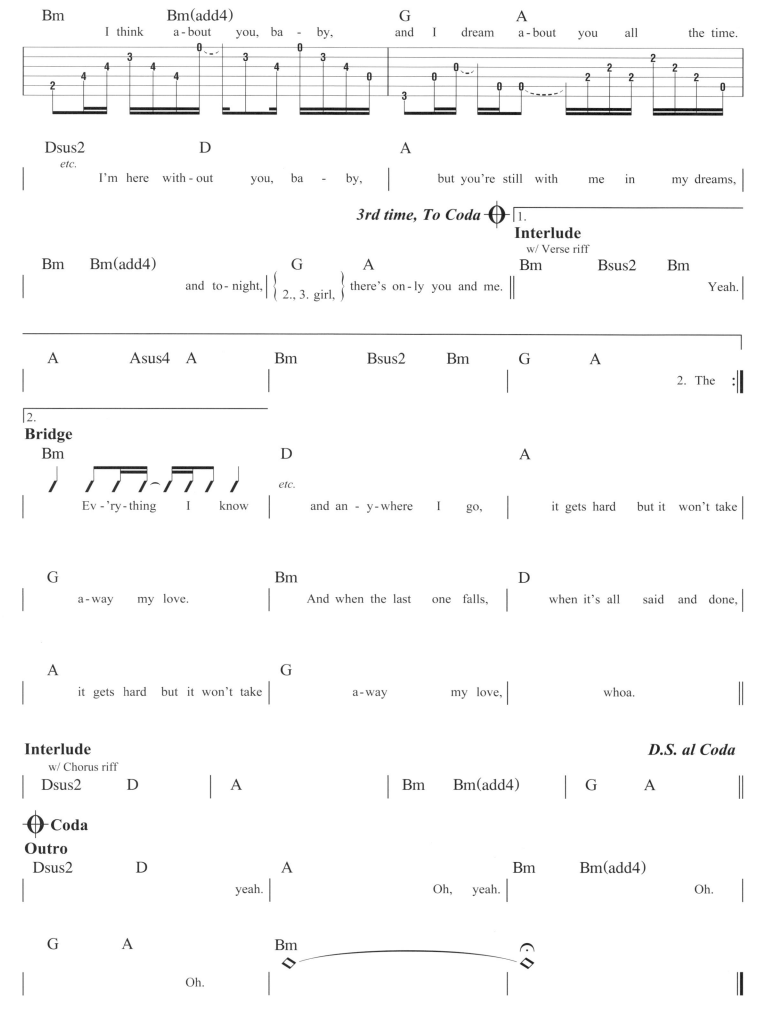

Hey Joe

Words and Music by Billy Roberts

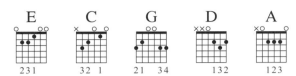

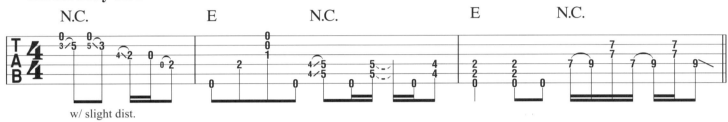

Key of E

Intro

Moderately slow

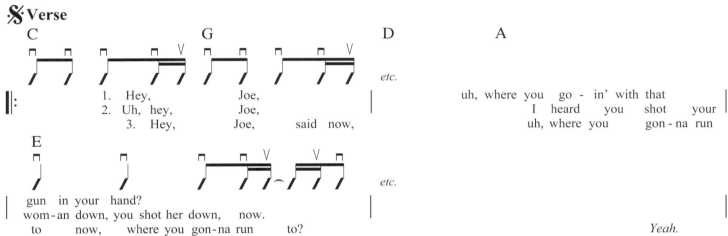

w/ slight dist.

Verse

C	G	D	A

1. Hey, Joe,
2. Uh, hey, Joe,
3. Hey, Joe, said now,

uh, where you go - in' with that
I heard you shot your
uh, where you gon - na run

E

gun in your hand?
wom-an down, you shot her down, now.
to now, where you gon-na run to?

Yeah.

C	G	D	A

Hey, Joe,
Uh, hey, Joe,
Hey, Joe, *I said,*

I said, where you go - in' with that gun
I heard you shot your old
where you gon - na run

E

in your hand? *Spoken: Al - right.*
la - dy down, you shot her down in the ground.
to now, where you, where you gon - na go?

Yeah!

Well, dig it!

*Lyrics in italics are spoken throughout.

C	G	D	A

I'm go - in' down to shoot my old la - dy,
Yes, I did, I shot her,
I'm go - in' way down south,

you know I caught her mess - in' 'round with an-oth-er
you know I caught her mess - in' 'round,
way down to

E

man.
mess - in' 'round town.
Mex - i - co way!

Yeah!

Al - right!

C	G	D	A

I'm go-in' down to shoot my old la-dy, | you know I caught her mess-in' 'round with an -
Uh, yes I did, I shot her, | you know I caught my old la-dy mess-in' 'round
I'm go-in' way down south, | way down where I

3rd time, To Coda ⊕

E			

oth-er man. *Huh!* *And that ain't* | *too* *cool.* *I shot her!*
town. *And I gave her the* | *gun,* *I shot her!*
can be free! Ain't no one | gon-na find me babe!

Guitar Solo

C	G	D	A	E

(Woo! | Ah! Hey, | Joe!) | *Al - right!* | *Shoot her one more time a - gain for me.*

C	G	D	A	E

(Oo, | | hey, | Joe!) | *Yeah!* | *Ah, dig it!*

Interlude

C	G	D	A

(Hey, | | Joe, | where you gon - na

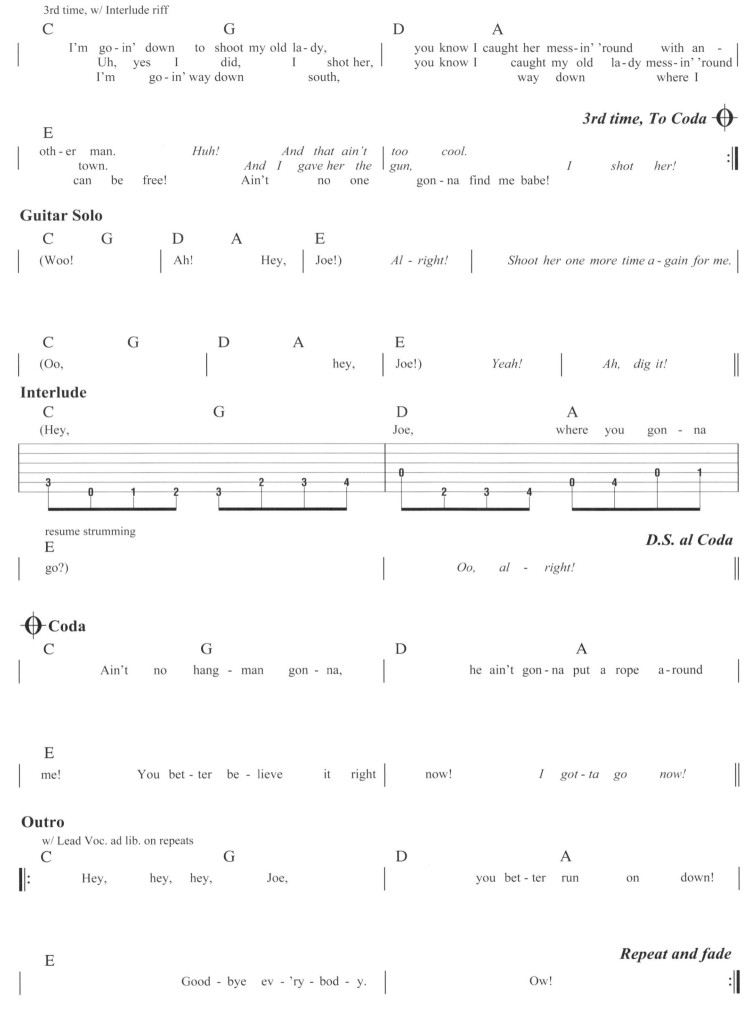

resume strumming

D.S. al Coda

E			

go?) | | *Oo, al - right!* |

⊕ Coda

C	G	D	A

Ain't no hang - man gon - na, | he ain't gon - na put a rope a - round |

E			

me! You bet - ter be - lieve it right | now! | *I got - ta go now!* |

Outro

w/ Lead Voc. ad lib. on repeats

C	G	D	A

‖: Hey, hey, hey, Joe, | you bet - ter run on down! |

Repeat and fade

E			

Good - bye ev - 'ry - bod - y. | *Ow!* :‖

Hide Away

By Freddie King and Sonny Thompson

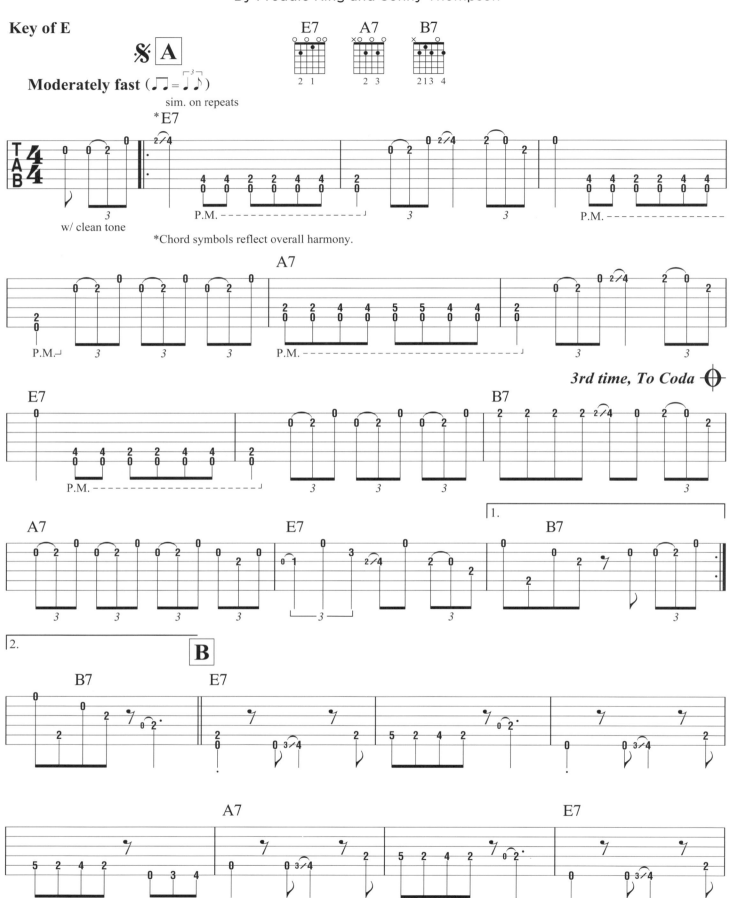

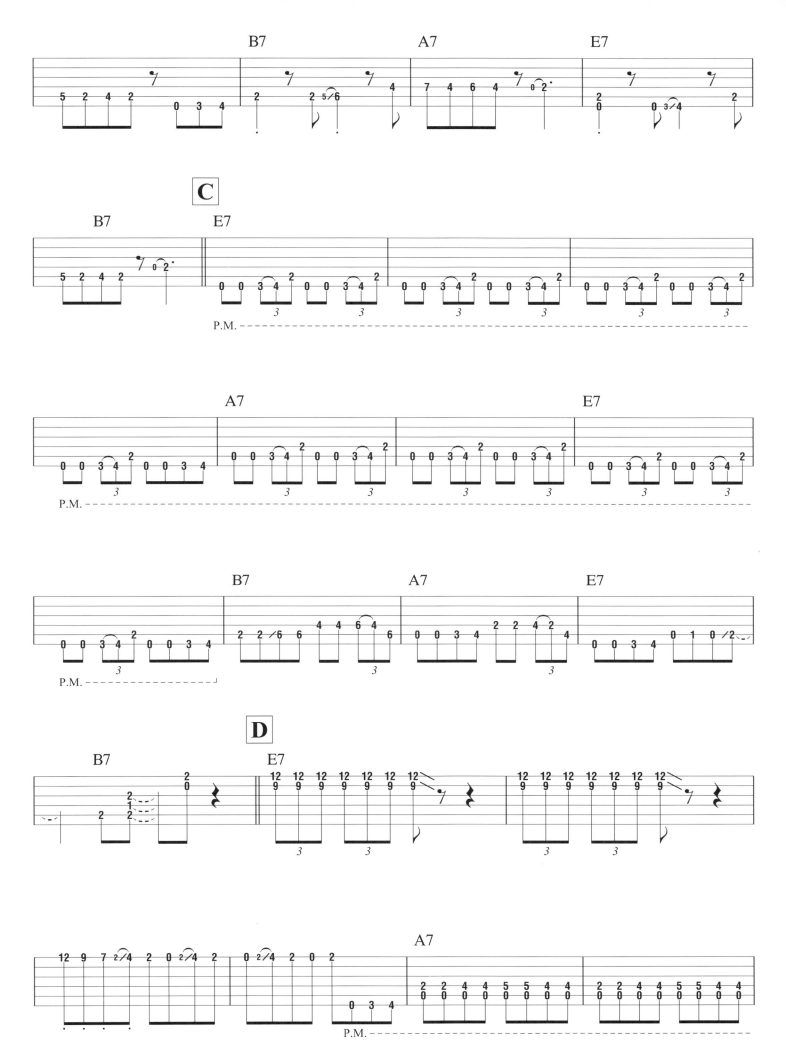

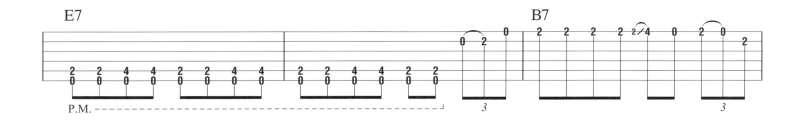

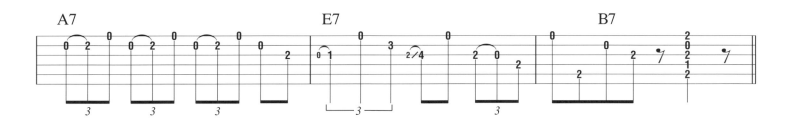

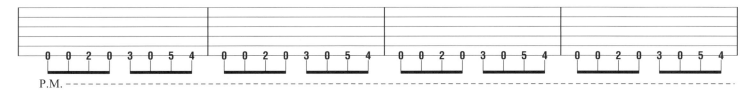

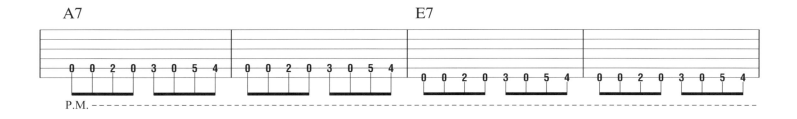

D.S. al Coda

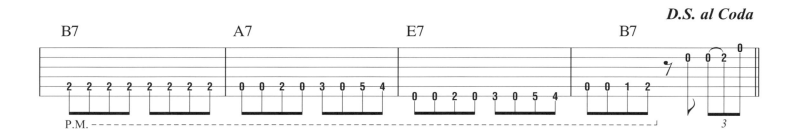

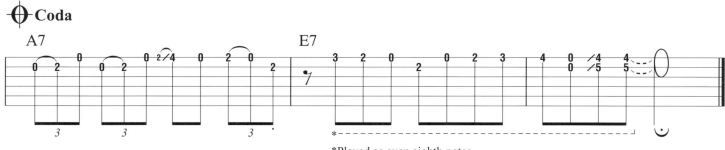

*Played as even eighth notes.

44

Knockin' on Heaven's Door

Words and Music by Bob Dylan

Key of G
Intro
Slow

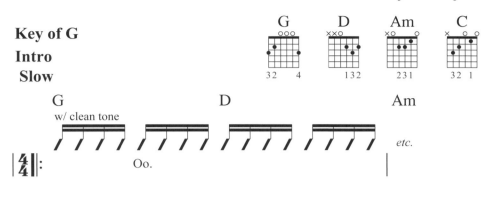

G   D   Am

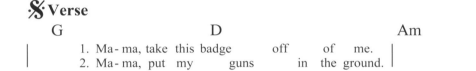

4/4 : Oo.

G   D   C

Oo.

Verse

G   D   Am

1. Ma-ma, take this badge   off   of me.
2. Ma-ma, put my   guns   in the ground.

G   D   C

I can't use it an - y - more.
I can't shoot them   an - y - more.

G   D   Am

It's get-tin' dark,   too dark for me to see. }
That long   black cloud is   com-in' down. }

G   D   C

I feel I'm knock - in' on heav-en's door.

Chorus

G   D   Am

: Knock, knock, knock- in' on heav-en's door.

4th time, To Coda ⊕ | 1. | 2.   **D.S. al Coda**
                                                                                        (take repeat)

G   D   C   C

Knock, knock, knock-in' on heav-en's door.

⊕ **Coda**   **Outro**   *Repeat and fade*

C   G   D   Am   G   D   C

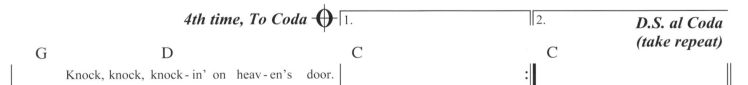

: Oo.   Oo.

The House of the Rising Sun

Words and Music by Alan Price

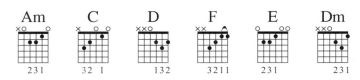

Am   C   D   F   E   Dm

Key of Am

Intro

Moderately slow, in 2

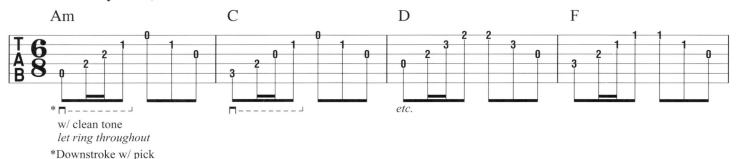

w/ clean tone
let ring throughout

*Downstroke w/ pick

etc.

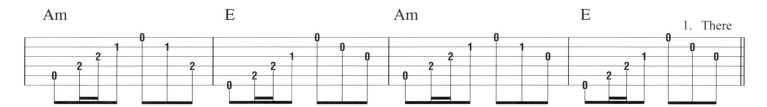

1. There

𝄋 Verse

1st - 3rd times, pick chords
4th time, strum chords
5th time, pick chords
6th & 7th times, strum chords

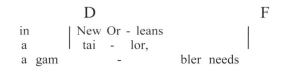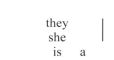

Am	C	D	F	
is a	house	in	New Or - leans	they
moth - er	was	a	tai - lor,	she
on - ly	thing	a gam -	bler needs	is a

4. *Organ Solo*
5. - 7. *See additional lyrics*

Am	C	E		
call the	Ris - ing Sun.			And it's
sewed my	new blue jeans.			My
suit - case and	a trunk.			And the

Am	C	D	F	
been the	ru - in	of	man - y a poor boy,	and
fa - ther	was	a	gam - blin' man	is
on - ly time	he's		sat - is - fied	is

Interlude

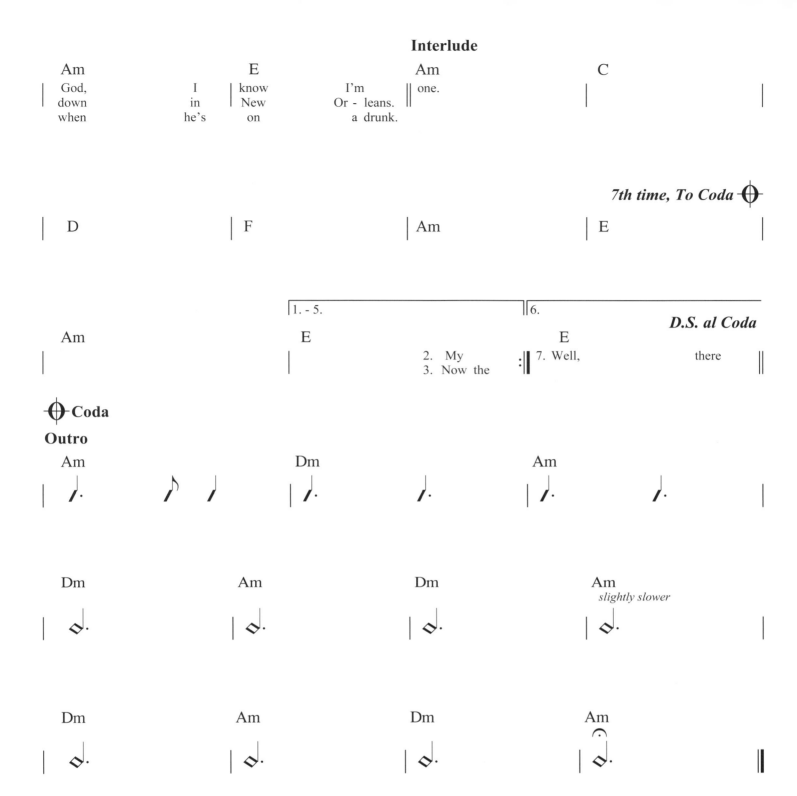

Coda

Outro

Additional Lyrics

5. Oh, mother, tell your children
   Not to do what I have done,
   Spend your lives in sin and misery
   In the House of the Rising Sun.

6. Well, I got one foot on the platform,
   The other foot on the train.
   I'm goin' back to New Orleans
   To wear that ball and chain.

7. Well, there is a house in New Orleans
   They call the Rising Sun.
   And it's been the ruin of many a poor boy,
   And God, I know I'm one.

(I Can't Get No) Satisfaction

Words and Music by Mick Jagger and Keith Richards

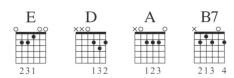

Key of E

Intro

Moderately fast

Chorus

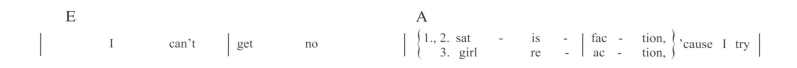

Refrain

Verse

D	A	E	D	A

1. When I'm **‖** driv - in' in my car | and the
2. When I'm **‖** watch - in' my T V | and a
3. When I'm rid - in' 'round the world, | and I'm

E	D	A	E

man come on the ra | - di - o; he's | tell - in' me more and more
man comes on and tells | me how | white my shirts can be.
do - in' this and I'm sign - in' that; and I'm | try - in' to make some girl,

D	A	E	D	A

a - bout some | use - less in - for - ma | - tion sup - posed to
But, he | can't be a man 'cause he | does - n't smoke the
who tells me, | ba - by, bet - ter come back | may - be next week. 'Cause you

E	D	A	E

fire my im - ag - in - a | - tion. I can't
same cig - a - rettes as me. | I can't } get no,
see I'm on a los - ing streak, I can't }

D	A	E	N.C.	E

oh, no, no, | no. | Hey, hey, hey.

1., 2. | *3.*

D	A	E	D	A	D	A

That's what I say. | **:‖** | I can't **‖**

Outro-Refrain

E	D	A	E	D	A

get no, | I can't | get no, | I can't

Repeat and fade

E	D	A	E	D	A

get no | sat - is - **‖:** fac - tion. | No sat - is - **:‖**

49

I Wanna Be Sedated

Words and Music by Jeffrey Hyman, John Cummings and Douglas Colvin

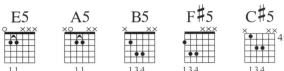

Key of E

Intro

Fast

E5

$\frac{4}{4}$ / / / / / / / / *etc.*

P.M. -

w/ dist.

Verse

E5 | 1., 2. Twen-ty, twen-ty, twen-ty-four | hours to go, | A5 | I wan-na be se-dat- |

E5 | - ed. | Noth-ing to do, no-where | to go, | |

Chorus

A5 | I wan-na be se-dat | E5 | - ed. Just | B5 | { get me to the air-port, / put me in a wheel-chair, |

E5 | put me on a plane. } / get me on a plane. } | B5 | Hur-ry, hur-ry, hur-ry, be- | E5 | fore I go in-sane. I |

B5 | can't con-trol my fin-gers, I | E5 | can't con-trol my brain, oh, | A5 | no, oh, oh, oh, |

1.

Interlude

B5 | oh. | E5 | | | |

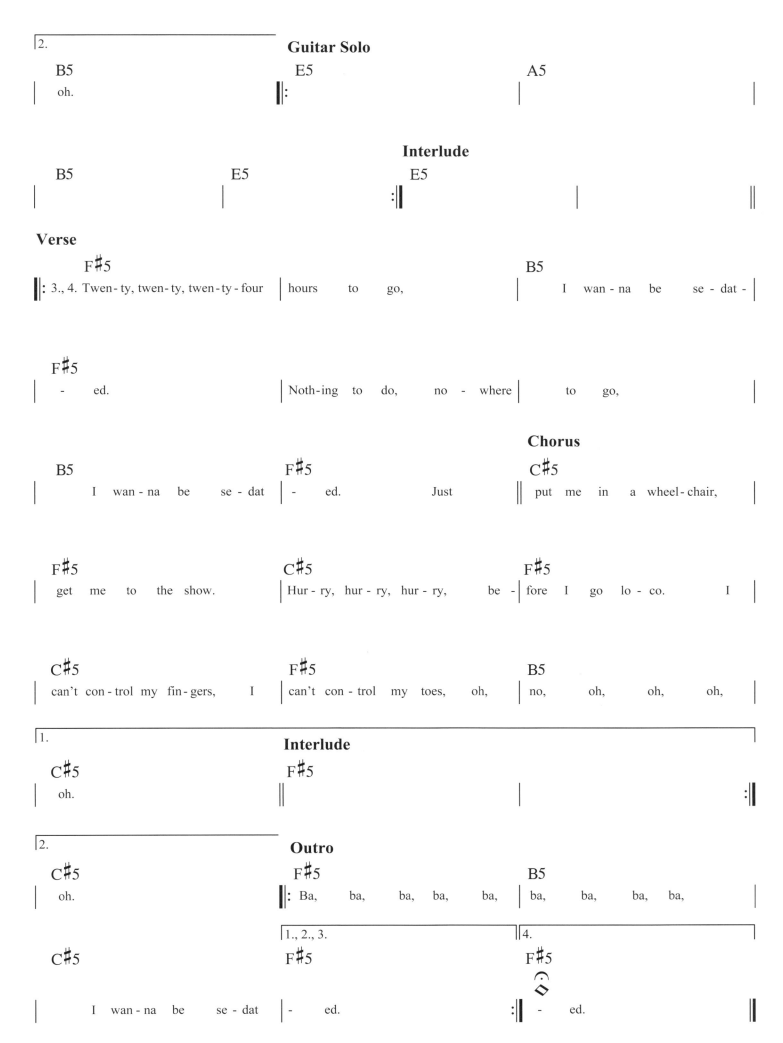

Guitar Solo

|2.

B5   E5   A5

oh.

Interlude

B5   E5   E5

Verse

F#5   B5

3., 4. Twen-ty, twen-ty, twen-ty-four | hours to go, | I wan-na be se-dat-

F#5

- ed. | Noth-ing to do, no-where | to go, |

Chorus

B5   F#5   C#5

I wan-na be se-dat | - ed. Just | put me in a wheel-chair, |

F#5   C#5   F#5

get me to the show. | Hur-ry, hur-ry, hur-ry, be- | fore I go lo-co. I |

C#5   F#5   B5

can't con-trol my fin-gers, I | can't con-trol my toes, oh, | no, oh, oh, oh, |

|1.   **Interlude**

C#5   F#5

oh.

|2.   **Outro**

C#5   F#5   B5

oh. | Ba, ba, ba, ba, ba, | ba, ba, ba, ba, |

|1., 2., 3. ||4.

C#5   F#5   F#5

I wan-na be se-dat | - ed. | - ed.

Iron Man

Words and Music by Frank Iommi, John Osbourne, William Ward and Terence Butler

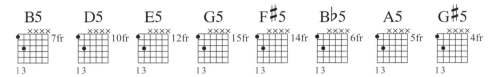

| B5 | D5 | E5 | G5 | F#5 | Bb5 | A5 | G#5 |

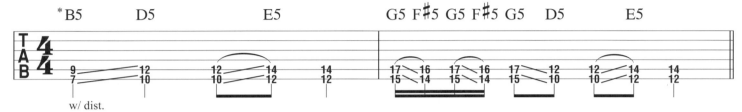

Key of Em

Intro

Slow

w/ dist.

*Chord symbols reflect implied harmony.

Verse

B5	D5	E5	G5 F#5 G5 F#5 G5 F#5	D5	E5
1. Has	he	lost his	mind?	Can	he see or is he blind?
2. Is	he	live or	dead?	I	see thoughts with-in his head.

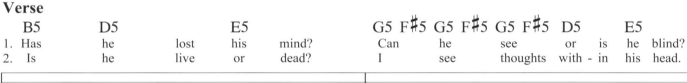

B5	D5	E5	G5 F#5 G5 F#5 G5	D5	E5
Can	he walk	at all,	or	if he moves will he fall?
We'll	just pass	him there.	Why	should we e-ven care?

Interlude

| B5 | D5 | B5 Bb5 A5 | G#5 A5 Bb5 | A5 | N.C. |

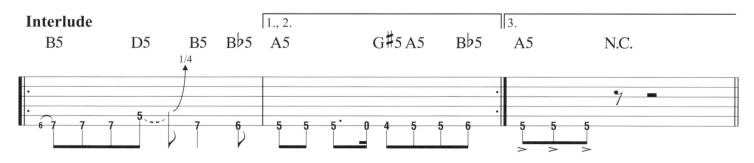

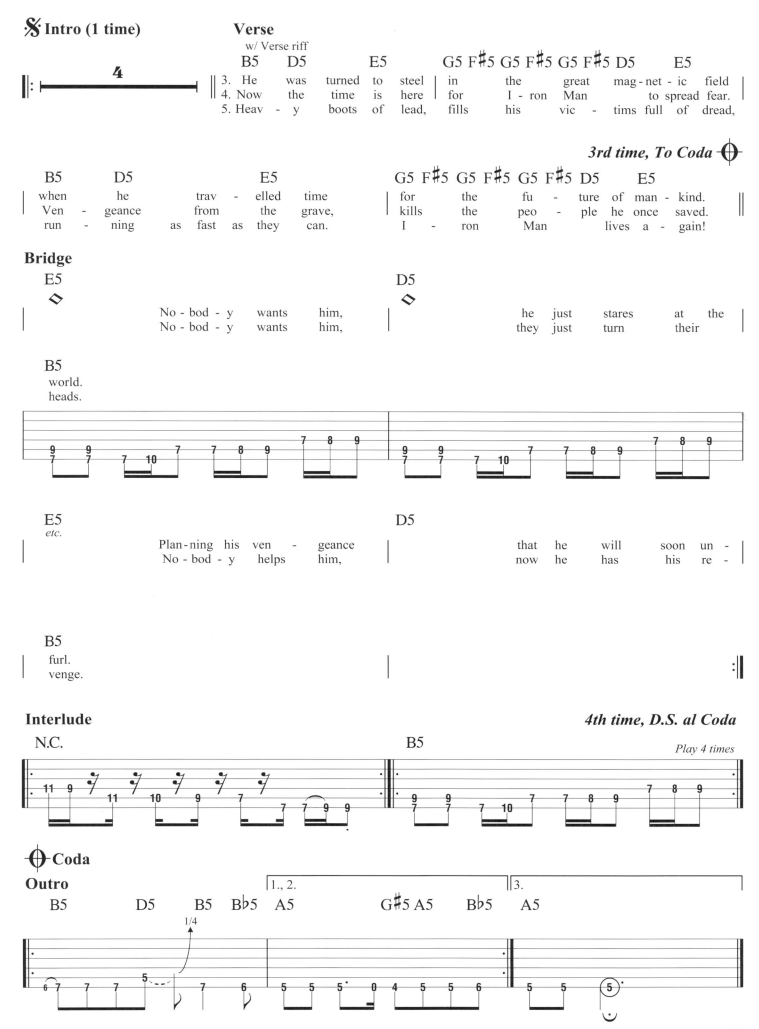

Island in the Sun

Words and Music by Rivers Cuomo

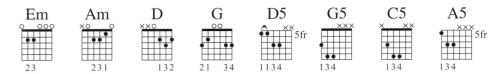

Em   Am   D   G   D5   G5   C5   A5

Key of G

Intro

Moderately

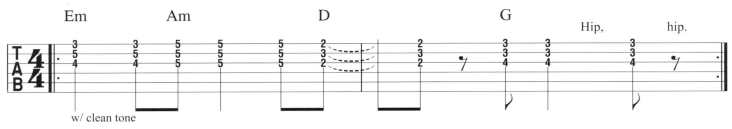

w/ clean tone

Hip,   hip.

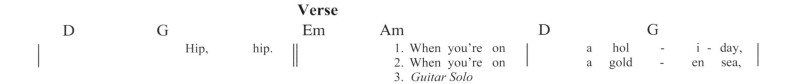

Hip,   hip.   *etc.*

Em   Am   D   G   Em   Am

Verse

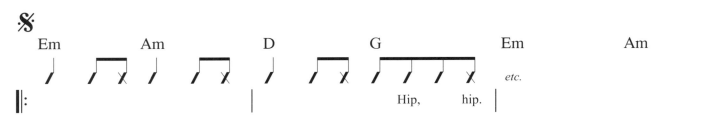

D   G   Em   Am   D   G

Hip,   hip.
1. When you're on ∥ a hol - i - day,
2. When you're on ∥ a gold - en sea,
3. *Guitar Solo*

Em   Am   D   G   Em   Am

you can't find | no words to say | all the things
you don't need | no mem - o - ry, | just a place

D   G   Em   Am   D   G

that come to you, | and I want | to feel it too.
to call your own | as we drift | in - to the zone.
Guitar Solo ends

Chorus

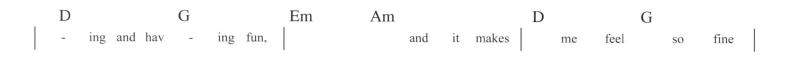

Em   Am   D   G   Em   Am

| On an is | - land in the sun, | we'll be play -

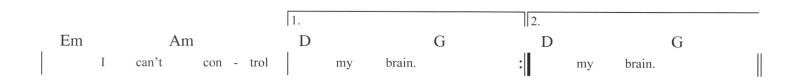

D   G   Em   Am   D   G

| - ing and hav - ing fun, | and it makes | me feel so fine |

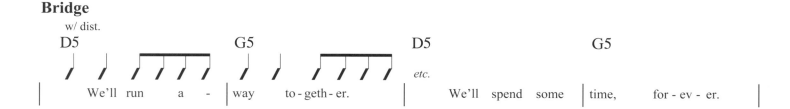

Em   Am   D   G   D   G

1. | I can't con - trol | my brain. :|| 2. my brain. ||

Bridge

w/ dist.

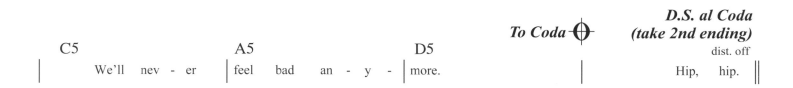

D5   G5   D5   G5

| We'll run a - | way to - geth - er. *etc.* | We'll spend some | time, for - ev - er. |

To Coda ⊕   ***D.S. al Coda (take 2nd ending)***

dist. off

C5   A5   D5

| We'll nev - er | feel bad an - y - | more. | Hip, hip. ||

⊕ **Coda**   **Outro**

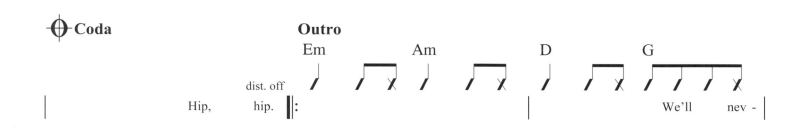

dist. off   Em   Am   D   G

| Hip, hip. ||: | We'll nev -

Repeat and fade

Em   Am   D   G   Em   Am   D   G

etc. | - er feel bad an | - y - more. | No, no. :||

Jailbreak

Words and Music by Philip Parris Lynott

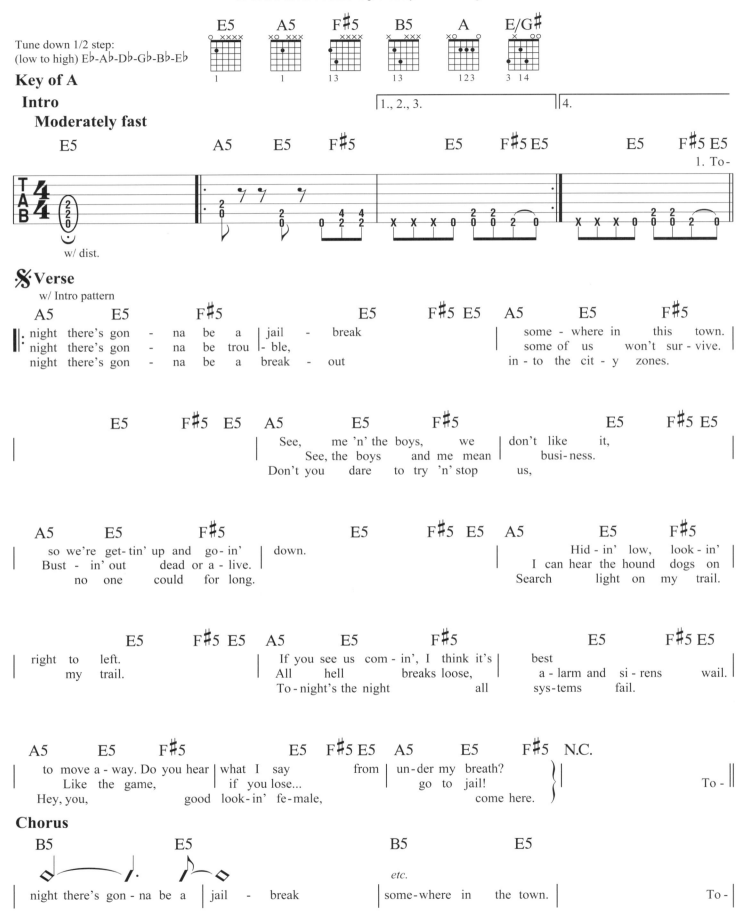

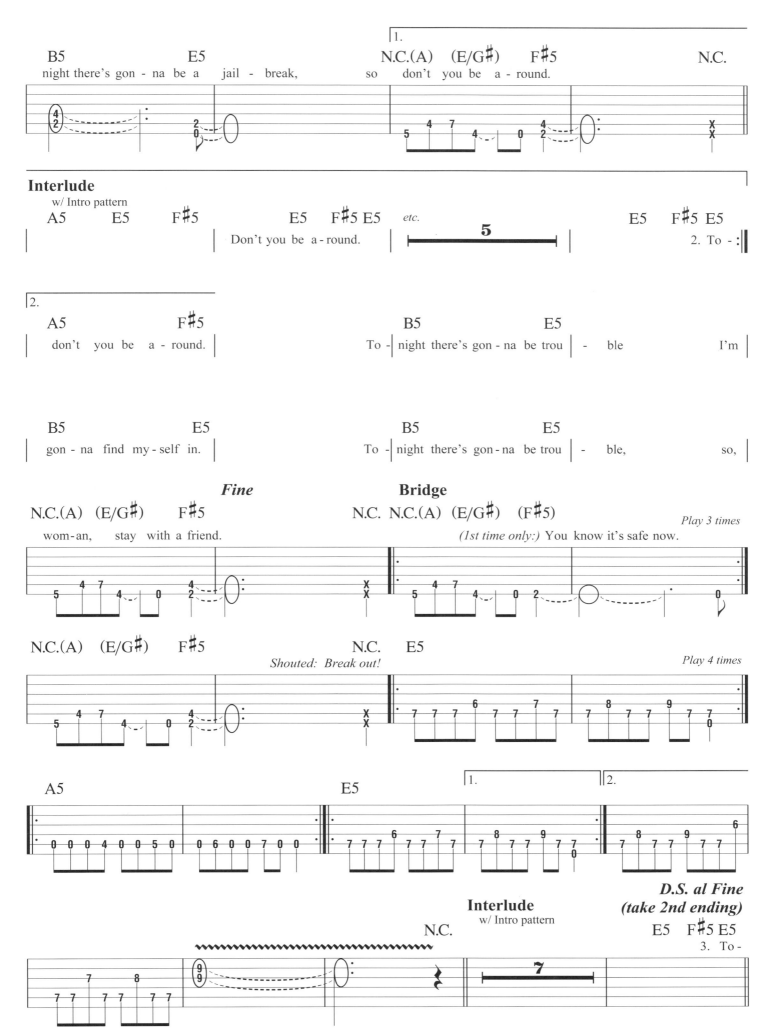

Mr. Jones

Words and Music by Adam Duritz, David Bryson, Charles Gillingham,
Matthew Malley, Steve Bowman, Daniel Vickrey and Ben Mize

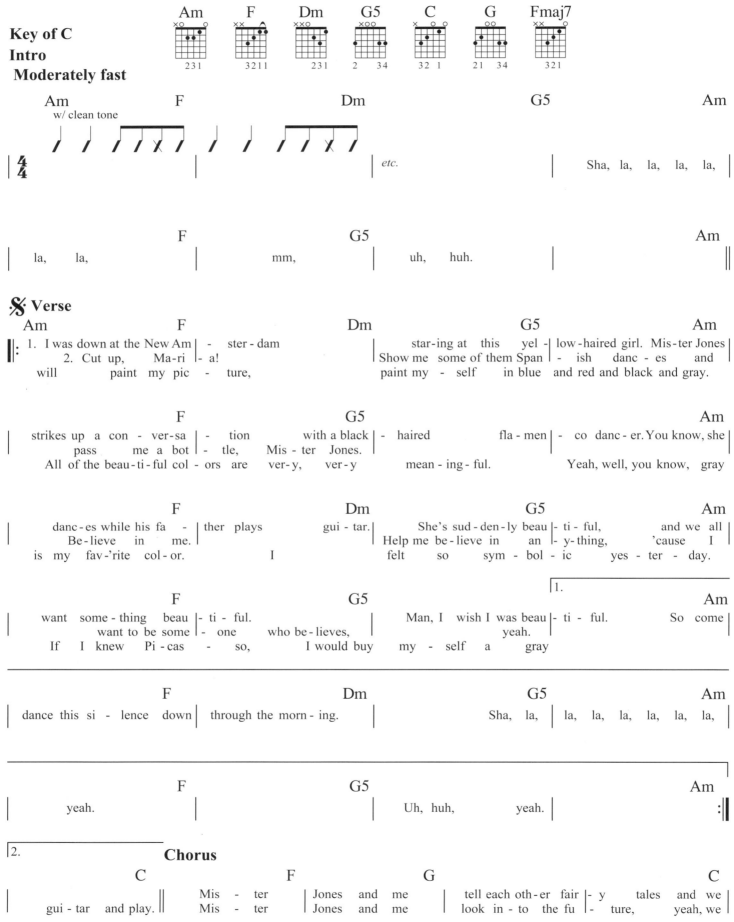

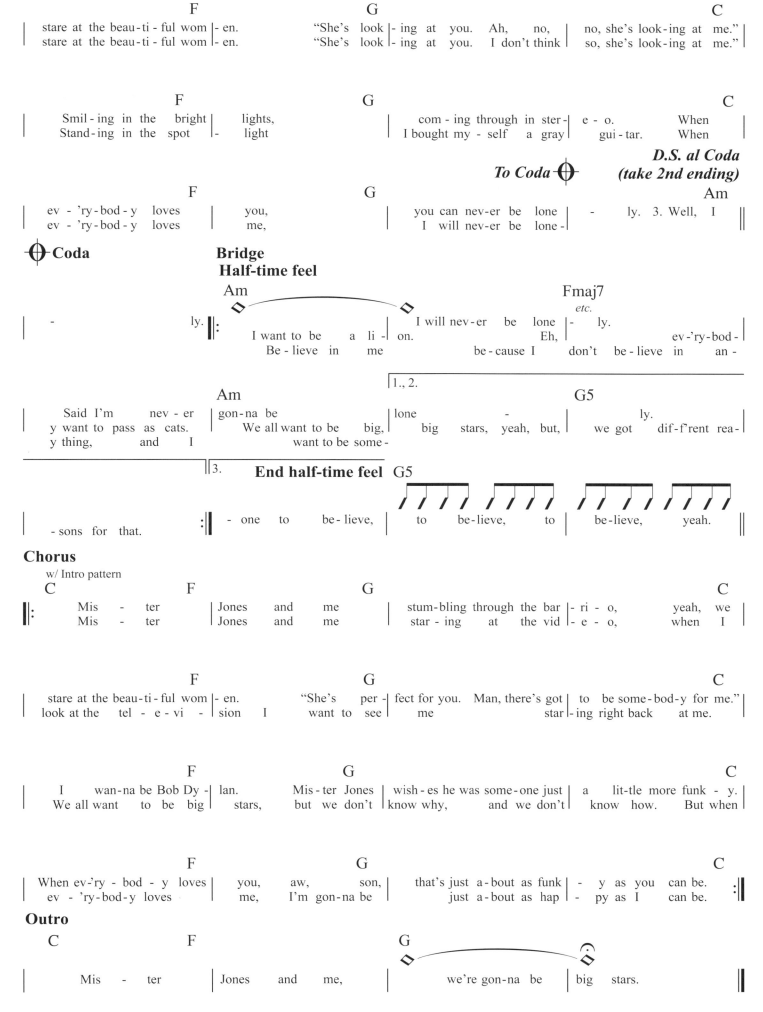

F   G   C

stare at the beau-ti-ful wom|-en.   "She's look|-ing at you. Ah, no, | no, she's look-ing at me."
stare at the beau-ti-ful wom|-en.   "She's look|-ing at you. I don't think | so, she's look-ing at me."

F   G   C

Smil-ing in the bright| lights, | com-ing through in ster-| e - o. When
Stand-ing in the spot|- light | I bought my-self a gray| gui-tar. When

To Coda ⊕   ***D.S. al Coda***
(take 2nd ending)

F   G   Am

ev-'ry-bod-y loves | you, | you can nev-er be lone | - ly. 3. Well, I
ev-'ry-bod-y loves | me, | I will nev-er be lone-| ly.

⊕ Coda   **Bridge**
Half-time feel

Am   Fmaj7
etc.

- | ly. ‖: I want to be a li-| on. I will nev-er be lone|- ly.
Be-lieve in me be-cause I don't be-lieve in an-

| Eh, | ev-'ry-bod-

⌐1., 2.

Am   G5

Said I'm nev-er | gon-na be | lone - | ly.
y want to pass as cats. We all want to be big, big stars, yeah, but, | we got dif-f'rent rea-
y thing, and I want to be some-

‖3.   **End half-time feel** G5

- sons for that. :‖ - one to be-lieve, | to be-lieve, to | be-lieve, yeah.

Chorus
w/ Intro pattern
C   F   G   C

‖: Mis - ter | Jones and me | stum-bling through the bar|-ri - o, yeah, we
Mis - ter | Jones and me | star-ing at the vid|-e - o, when I

F   G   C

stare at the beau-ti-ful wom|-en. "She's per-|fect for you. Man, there's got| to be some-bod-y for me."
look at the tel-e-vi-|sion I want to see| me star|-ing right back at me.

F   G   C

I wan-na be Bob Dy-| lan. Mis-ter Jones | wish-es he was some-one just| a lit-tle more funk-y.
We all want to be big| stars, but we don't| know why, and we don't| know how. But when

F   G   C

When ev-'ry-bod-y loves | you, aw, son, | that's just a-bout as funk|- y as you can be. :‖
ev-'ry-bod-y loves | me, I'm gon-na be | just a-bout as hap|- py as I can be.

Outro
C   F   G

Mis - ter | Jones and me, | we're gon-na be | big stars. ‖

My Hero

Words and Music by Nate Mendel, Pat Smear and David Grohl

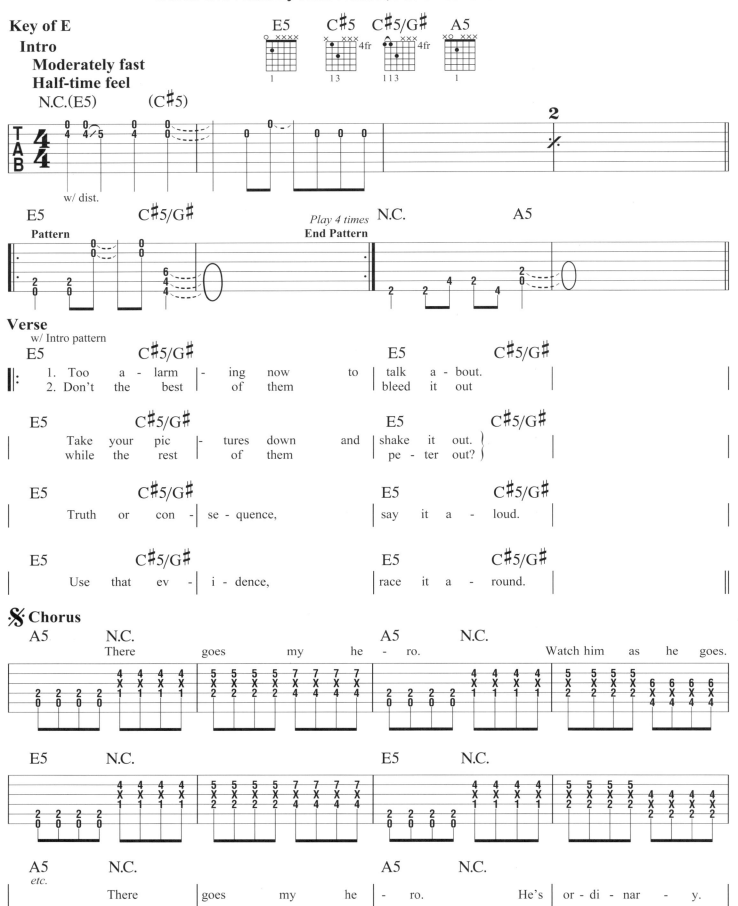

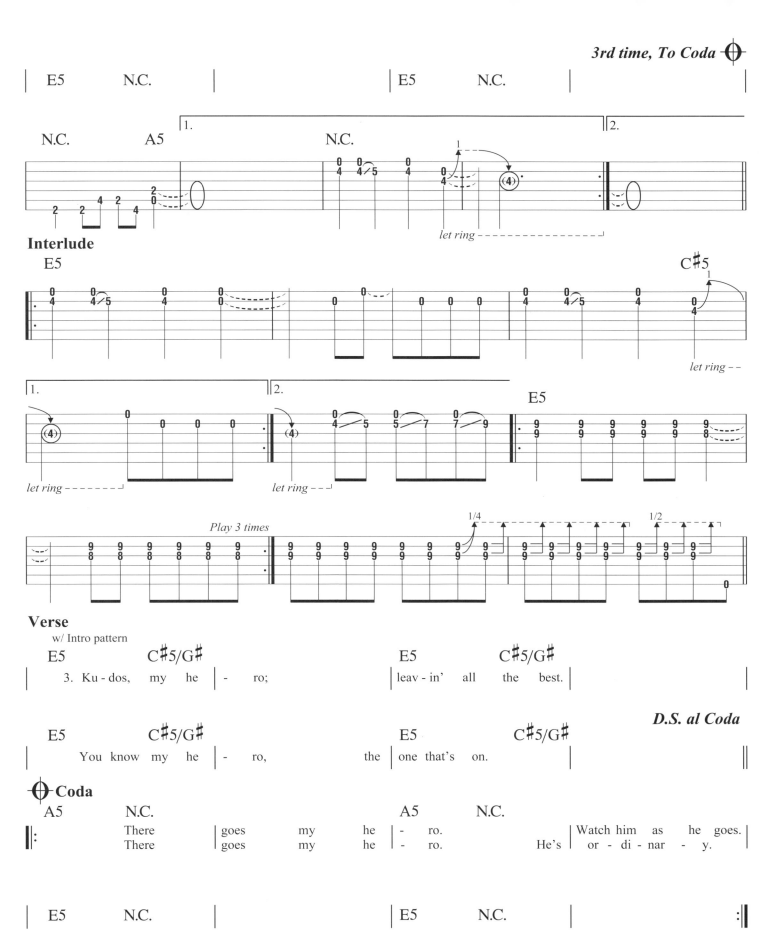

Interlude

Verse

w/ Intro pattern

E5		C#5/G#		E5		C#5/G#	
	3. Ku - dos,	my	he	- ro;	leav - in'	all	the best.

D.S. al Coda

E5		C#5/G#		E5		C#5/G#	
	You know	my	he	- ro,	the	one that's	on.

⊕ **Coda**

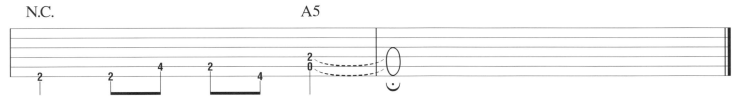

A5	N.C.				A5	N.C.		
There	goes	my	he	- ro.			Watch him as	he goes.
There	goes	my	he	- ro.	He's	or - di - nar	- y.	

No Rain

Words and Music by Blind Melon

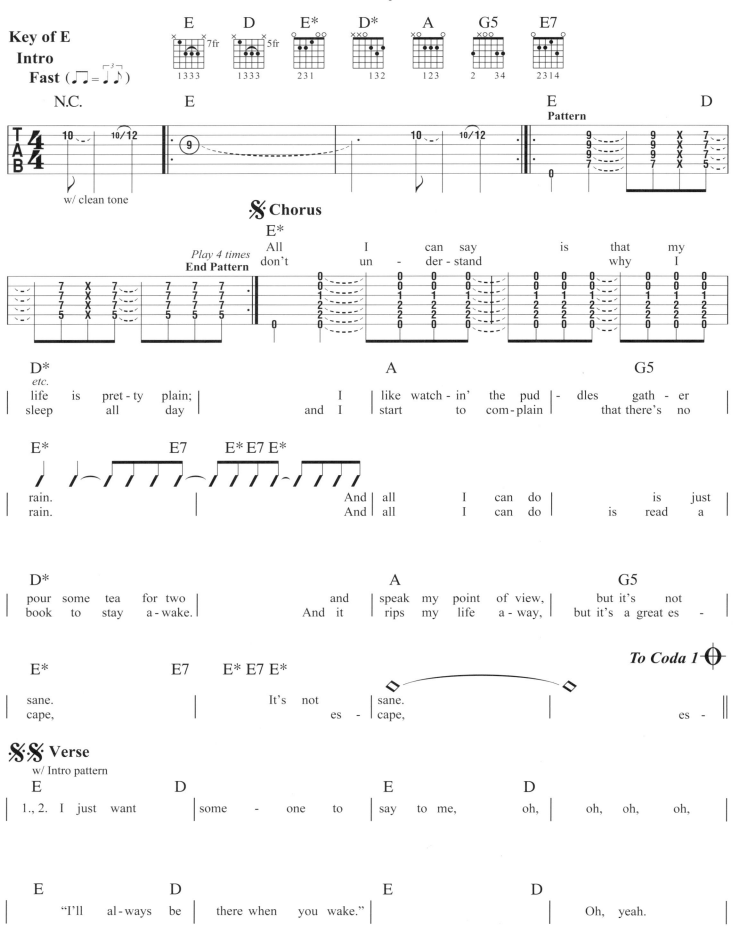

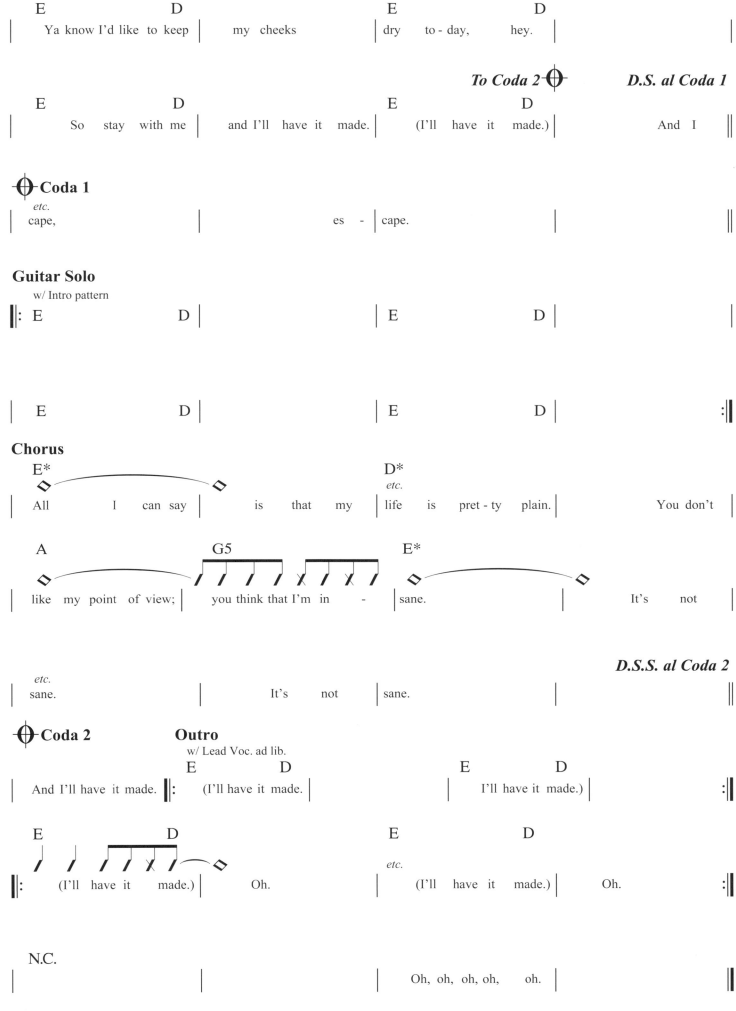

E		D		E		D	
Ya know I'd like to keep			my cheeks	dry to - day,	hey.		

To Coda 2 ⊕   *D.S. al Coda 1*

E		D		E		D	
So stay with me		and I'll have it made.		(I'll have it made.)		And I	

⊕ **Coda 1**

etc.
cape,   es - cape.

Guitar Solo
w/ Intro pattern

‖: E   D | | E   D | |

| E   D | | E   D | :‖

Chorus

E*   D*
etc.
All   I   can say   is   that   my   life   is   pret - ty   plain.   You don't

A   G5   E*
like   my   point   of view;   you think   that   I'm   in -   sane.   It's   not

D.S.S. al Coda 2

etc.
sane.   It's   not   sane.

⊕ **Coda 2**   **Outro**
w/ Lead Voc. ad lib.

E	D		E	D	
And I'll have it made. ‖: (I'll have it made. | | I'll have it made.) | | :‖

E   D   E   D
etc.
‖: (I'll have it made.)   Oh.   (I'll have it made.)   Oh.   :‖

N.C.
Oh, oh, oh, oh,   oh.

63

Oh, Pretty Woman

Words and Music by Roy Orbison and Bill Dees

Otherside

Words and Music by Anthony Kiedis, Flea, John Frusciante and Chad Smith

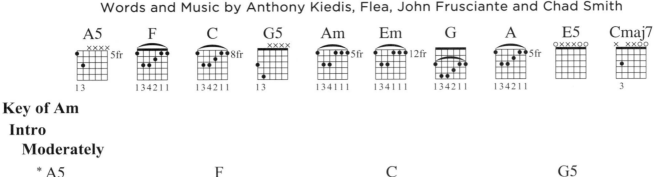

Key of Am

Intro

Moderately

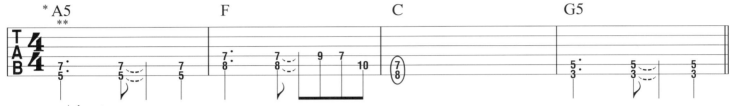

w/ clean tone

*Chord symbols reflect implied harmony.
**Bass & gtr. arr. for gtr., next 4 meas.

Chorus

w/ Intro riff

A5	F	C	G5
How long, how	long will I	slide,	sep - ar - ate my

A5	F	C	G5
side?		I don't,	I don't be - lieve it's

3rd time, To Coda

A5	F	C	G5
bad;		slit- tin' my throat, it's all	I ev - er...

Verse

Am ... Em ... Am

1. I heard your voice through a pho - to - graph; I thought it up, it brought
3. Pour my life in - to a pa - per cup; the ash - tray's full and I'm

etc.

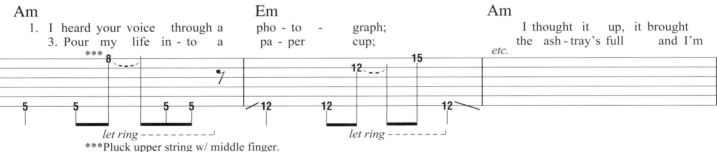

let ring

***Pluck upper string w/ middle finger.

Em ... Am ... Em

up the past. Once you know you can nev - er go back. } I've got to
spil - lin' my guts. She wants to know am I still a slut. }

G ... A

take it on the oth - er side.

Verse

w/ Verse riff

Am ... Em ... Am

2. Cen - tu - ries are what it meant to me; a cem - e - ter - y where I
4. Scar - let star - let and she's in my bed, a can - di - date, a, for my

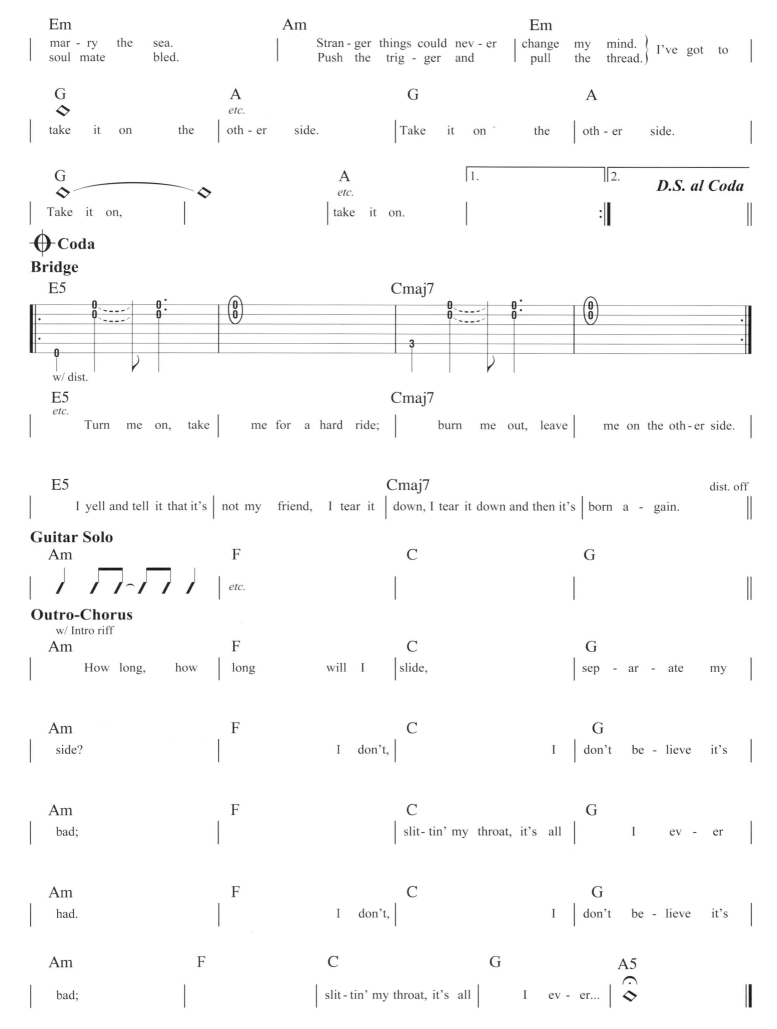

Peter Gunn

Theme Song from the Television Series
By Henry Mancini

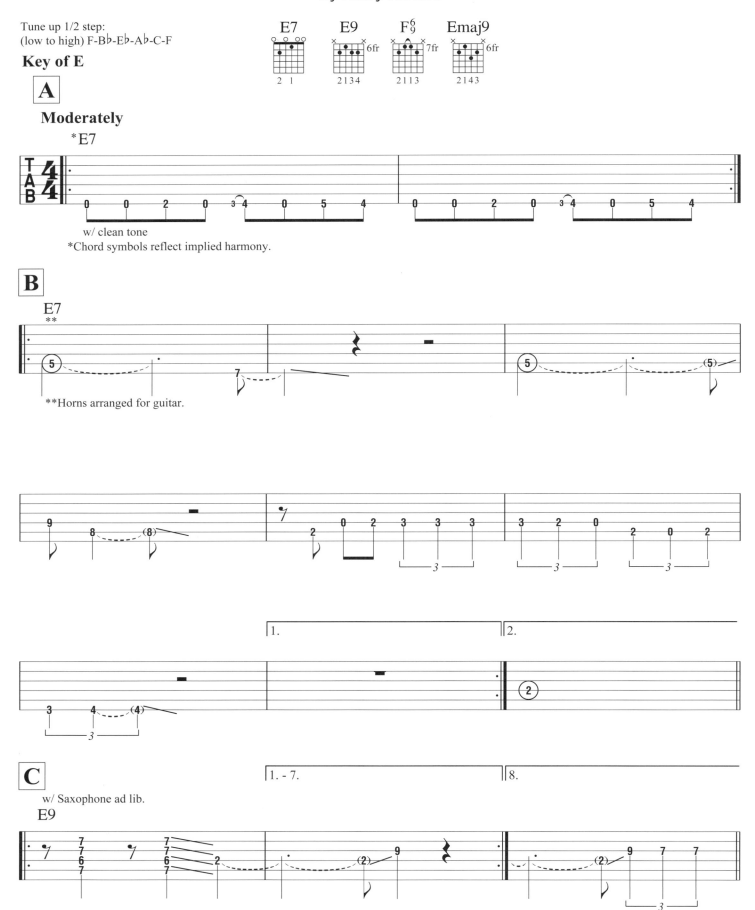

D

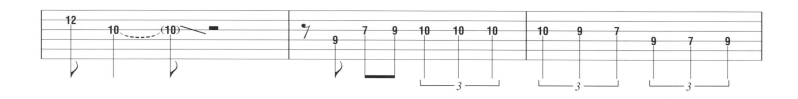

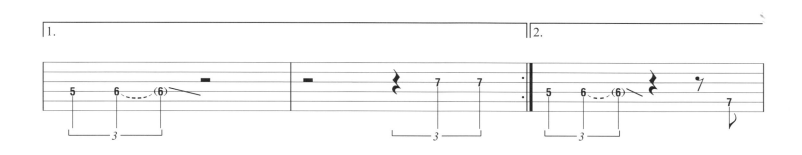

Plush

Words and Music by Scott Weiland, Dean DeLeo, Robert DeLeo and Eric Kretz

G5 Bb°7 Cm6 G D/F# F C/E Ebmaj7

D5 Csus2 G/B F/C G5* F5 Eb D

Key of G

Intro

Slow

|1., 2., 3.| |4.|

G5   Bb°7   Cm6   G   Cm6   G

w/ dist.

Verse

G   D/F#   F   C/E

1. And   I   feel   that time's   a wast - ed go,
2. And   I   feel   so much   de - pends   on the weath - er,

Ebmaj7   F   G   D/F#

so where   you   go - ing to to - mor - row? And   I   see   that these
so   is   it   rain - ing in your bed - room? And   I   see   that

F   C/E   Ebmaj7   F

are lies   to come,   so would   you   e - ven care?
these   are the eyes   of dis - ar - ray,

Pre-Chorus

D5   Csus2   G/B   Csus2   D5   Csus2   G/B   Csus2

And   I   feel   it,

D5   Csus2   G/B   Csus2   D5   Csus2   G/B   Csus2

and   I   feel   it.
and   she   feels   it.

𝄋 Chorus

Ebmaj7   F/C

Where   you   go - in' for to - mor -   row?

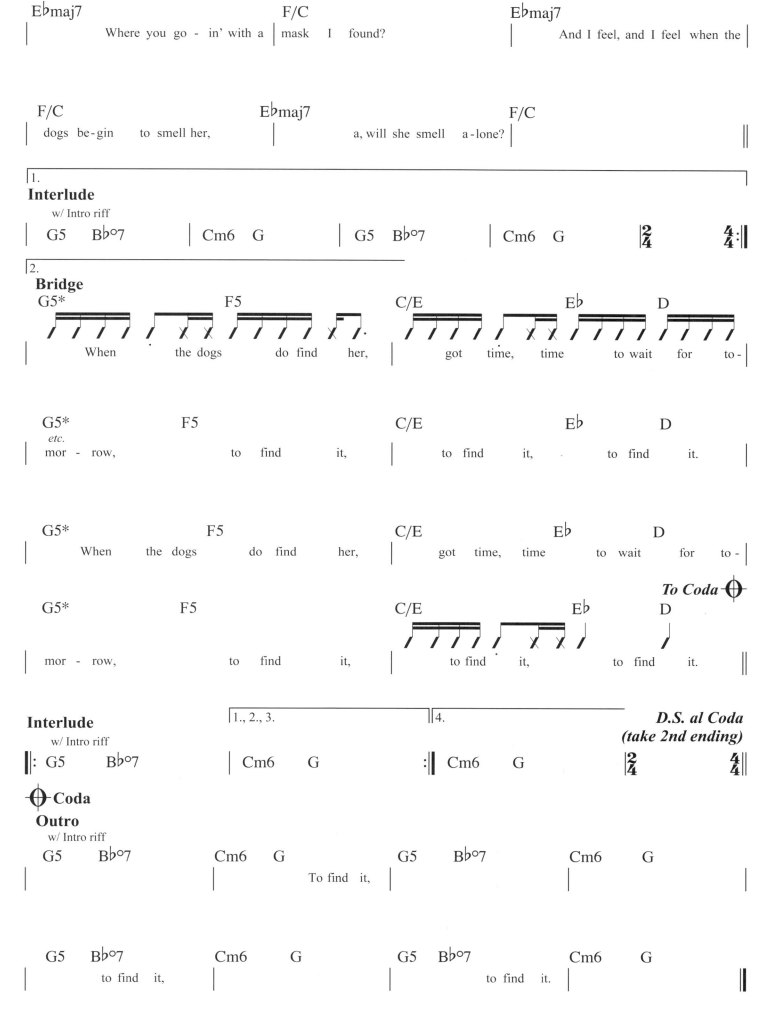

Eᵇmaj7 — Where you go-in' with a | mask I found?   F/C

Eᵇmaj7 — And I feel, and I feel when the |

F/C — dogs be-gin to smell her,   Eᵇmaj7 — a, will she smell a-lone?   F/C ‖

1.
Interlude
w/ Intro riff

| G5 Bᵇ°7 | Cm6 G | G5 Bᵇ°7 | Cm6 G | 2/4 | 4/4 :‖

2.
Bridge

G5* — When the dogs do find her,   F5   C/E — got time, time to wait for to-   Eᵇ   D

G5* — mor-row, to find it,   F5   C/E — to find it, to find it.   Eᵇ   D

G5* — When the dogs do find her,   F5   C/E — got time, time to wait for to-   Eᵇ   D

To Coda ⊕

G5* — mor-row, to find it,   F5   C/E — to find it, to find it.   Eᵇ   D ‖

Interlude
w/ Intro riff

1., 2., 3.

4.

D.S. al Coda
(take 2nd ending)

‖: G5 Bᵇ°7 | Cm6 G :‖ Cm6 G | 2/4 | 4/4 ‖

⊕ **Coda**
Outro
w/ Intro riff

G5 Bᵇ°7   Cm6 G — To find it,   G5 Bᵇ°7   Cm6 G

G5 Bᵇ°7   Cm6 G — to find it,   G5 Bᵇ°7   Cm6 G — to find it. ‖

Pride and Joy

Written by Stevie Ray Vaughan

Tune down 1/2 step:
(low to high) Eb-Ab-Db-Gb-Bb-Eb

Key of E

Intro

Moderately

E | A7 | B7 | E7 | B9 | E7#9

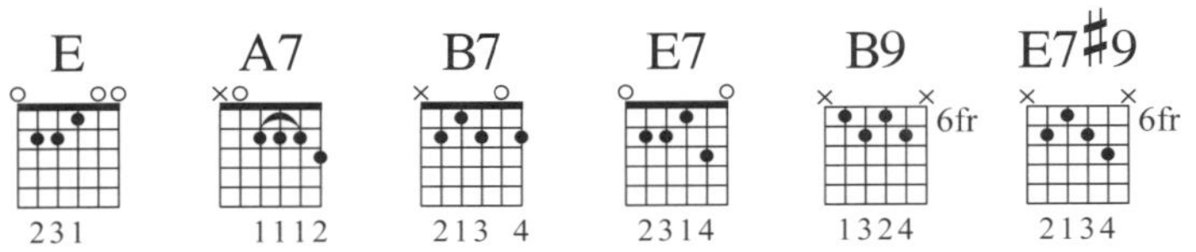

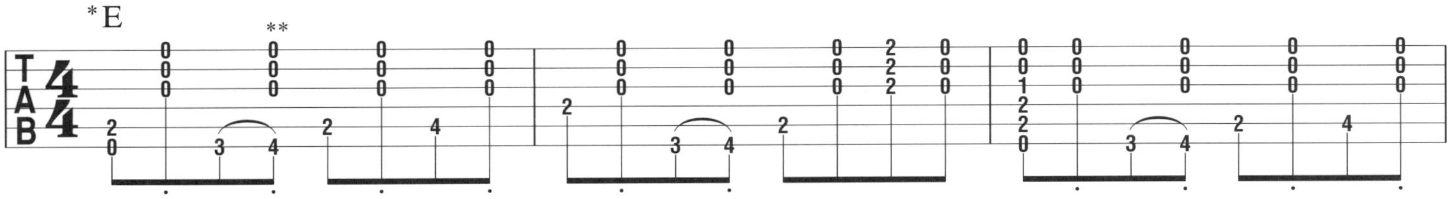

w/ dist.

*Chord symbols reflect implied harmony.

**Staccato applies to strings 1-3 only.

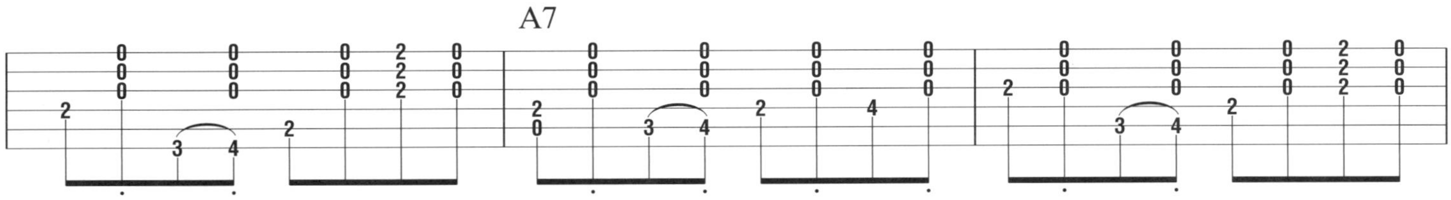

A7

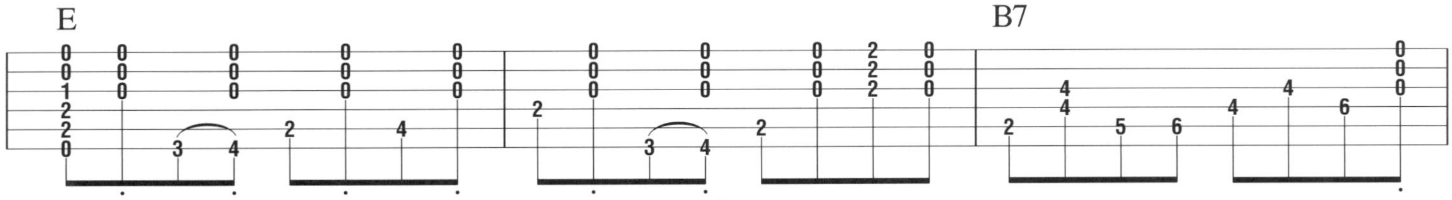

E | B7

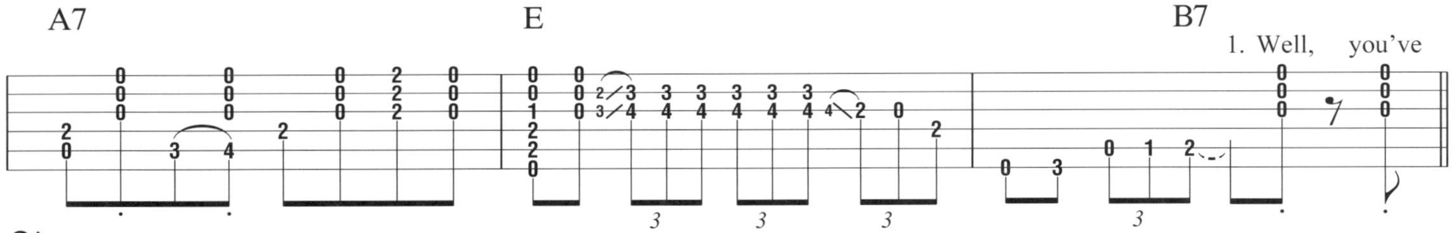

A7 | E | B7

1. Well,   you've

Verse

E

‖: heard a-bout lov-in' giv-in' sight   to   the   blind.   My ba-by's lov-in' cause the sun

2nd time, Guitar Solo
5. *See additional lyrics*

A7

to   shine.   An' she's my | sweet   lit-tle   thang,   she's   my

E | B7

pride   and   joy. | She's   my | sweet lit-tle ba-by,   I'm

A7 | E | B7

her   lit-tle   lov-er   boy. | 2. Yeah,   I ‖

Verse

E
| love my ba - by, my | heart and soul. | Love like ours a, won't nev - |
2nd & 3rd times, Guitar Solo

                    A7
| - er grow old. She's my | sweet lit - tle thang, | she's my |

E   B7
| pride and joy. | She's my | sweet lit - tle ba - by, I'm |

3rd time, To Coda ⊕

A7   E   B7
| her lit - tle lov - er boy. | | 3. Yeah, I |
                                                                    Guitar Solo ends 4. Well, I |

Verse

E N.C.   E N.C.   E N.C.
| love my la - dy, she's | long and lean. | You mess with her, you'll see a |
| love my ba - by, like the | fin - est a, wine. | Stick with her un - til the |

E7   A7
| man get - tin' mean. She's my | sweet lit - tle thang, ⎫ | she's my |
| end of time. An' she's my | sweet lit - tle thang, ⎭ | |

E   B7
| pride and joy. | She's my | sweet lit - tle ba - by, I'm |

                                               1.   2.   ***D.S. al Coda***

A7   E   B7   B7
| her lit - tle lov - er boy. | | : ‖ | 5. Yeah, I ‖

⊕ **Coda**

E   B9 E7♯9   N.C.

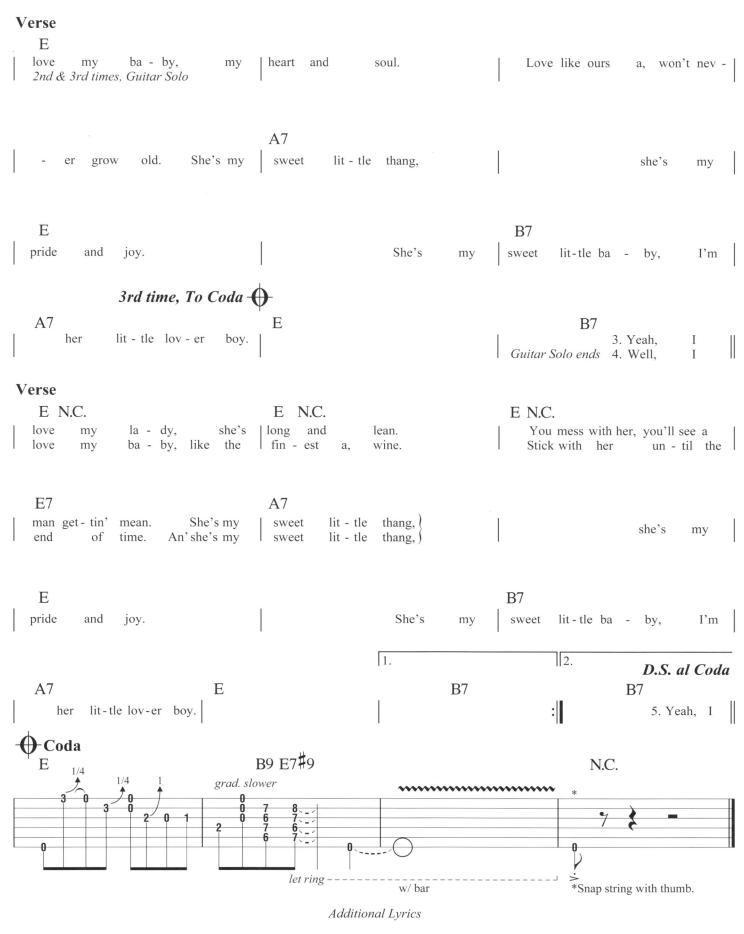

grad. slower   *let ring* - - - - - - - - - - - -   *w/ bar*   *Snap string with thumb.*

Additional Lyrics

5. Yeah, I love my baby, my heart and soul.
   Love like ours, ah, won't never grow old.
   She's my sweet little thang,
   She's my pride and joy.
   She's my sweet little baby,
   I'm her little lover boy.

Runnin' Down a Dream

Words and Music by Tom Petty, Jeff Lynne and Mike Campbell

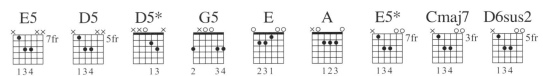

Key of E

Intro

Fast

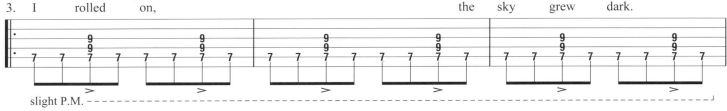

w/ slight dist.

Verse

	beau-ti-ful	day,		the	sun	beat	down.
	felt	so	good,	like	an-y-thing was	pos-si-ble.
3. I	rolled	on,		the	sky	grew	dark.

slight P.M.

etc.			I	had	the	ra-di-o	on.		I was driv-
	Hit	cruise	con-trol,		and rubbed my
	I	put the	ped-al	down		to make some

E5

-in'.			The	trees	went	by,
eyes.			The	last	three	days,
time.		There's	some-thin'	good

	me and	Del	were	sing-in'		lit-tle
	and the rain	was un-stop-pa-ble,		it was
	wait-in' down this road.		I'm

D5 .... E5

"Run-a-way,"		I was	fly-in'.		Yeah,
al-ways cold,		no sun-shine.		Yeah,
pick-in' up		what-ev-er's	mine.		I'm

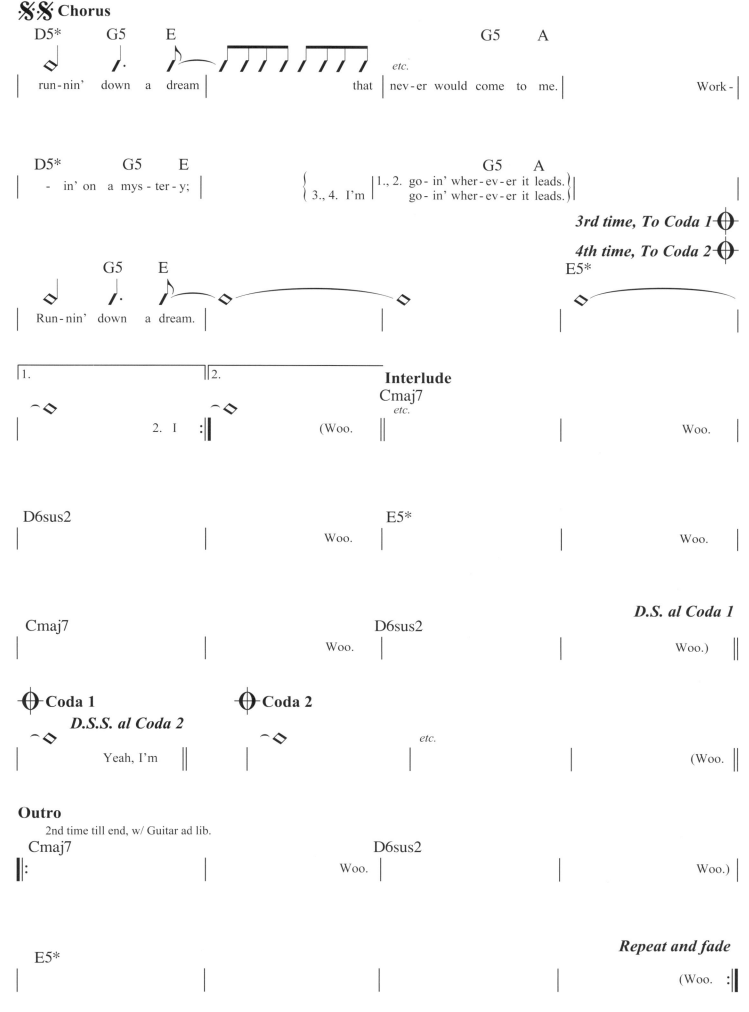

Santeria

Words and Music by Brad Nowell, Eric Wilson and Floyd Gaugh

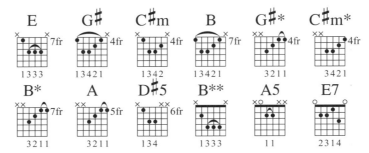

Key of E

Intro

Moderately slow

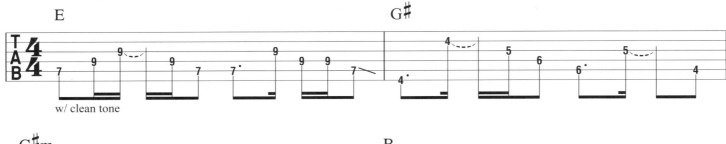

w/ clean tone

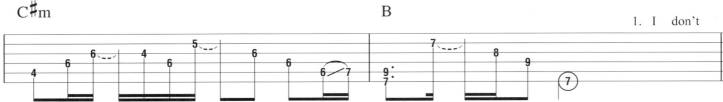

1. I don't

Verse

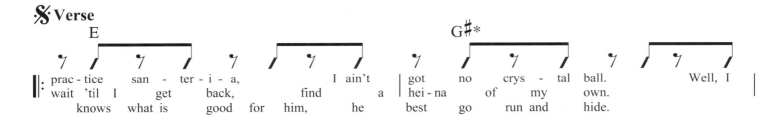

|: prac - tice san - ter - i - a,   I ain't | got no crys - tal ball.   Well, I
wait 'til I get back,   find a | hei - na of my own.
knows what is good for him,   he | best go run and hide.

had a mil - lion dol - lars but I, | I'd spend it all.   If
Dad - dy's gon - na love one and | all.   I
Dad - dy's got a new for - ty - | five   and

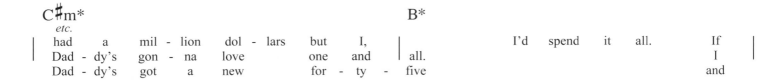

I could find that hei - na and that | San - cho that she's found,   well, I'd
feel the break, feel the break, feel | the break and I got to live it out,
I won't think twice to stick that bar - rel | straight down San - cho's throat.   Be -

pop a cap in San - cho and I'd | slap her down. :|
oh,   yeah, | huh. Well, I swear that I,
lieve me when I say that I | got some - thing for his punk ass.

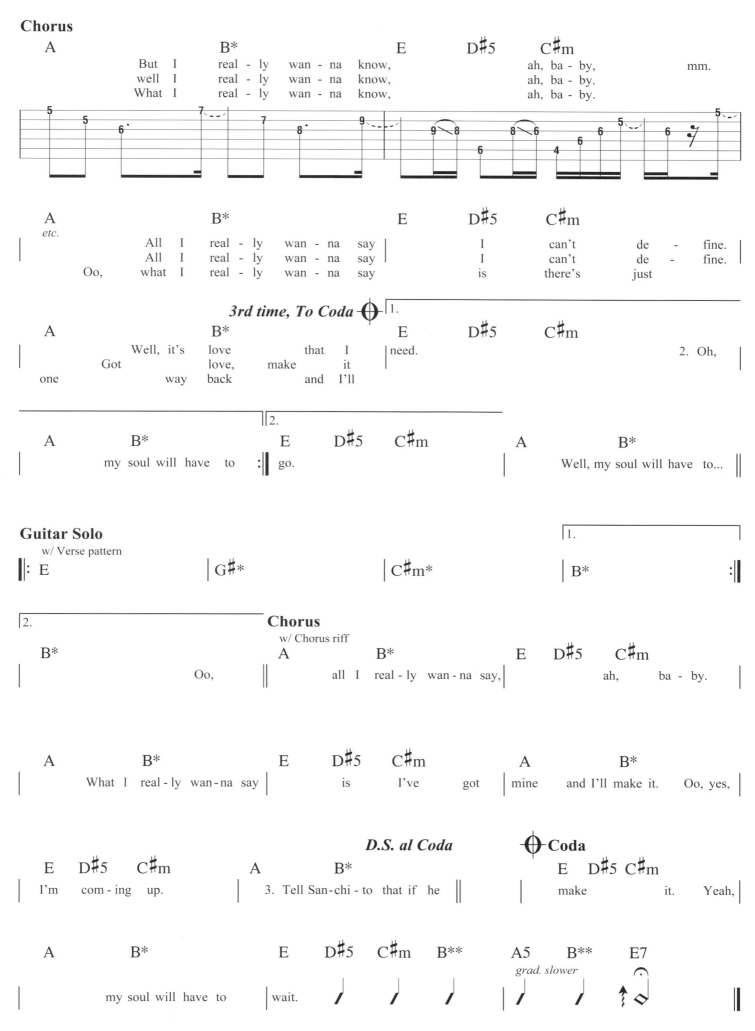

Seven Nation Army

Words and Music by Jack White

Open A tuning:
(low to high) E-A-E-A-C#-E

Key of E

G5   A   E   G   D   C   B

Intro

Moderately

N.C.

1. I'm gon-na

w/ slight dist.
w/ octave pedal, set for one octave below

§ Verse

w/ Intro riff

N.C.

fight 'em off,		a sev - en na - tion	ar - my could - n't hold me back.
hear a - bout it,		ev - 'ry sin - gle	one's got a sto - ry to
Wich - i - ta,		far from this	op - er - a for - ev - er - more.

	They're gon - na	rip it off,	tak - ing their	
tell.	Ev - 'ry - one	knows a - bout it	from the Queen of	
	I'm gon - na	work the straw,	make the sweat	

	time right be - hind my	back.	And I'm	talk - ing to my - self at night
Eng - land to the hounds of	hell.	And if I	catch it com - ing back my way
drip out of ev - 'ry	pore.	And I'm	bleed - ing, and I'm bleed - ing, and I'm

	be - cause I can't for - get.		
	I'm gon - na serve it to you.		And
bleed - ing right be - fore the Lord.		All the

Back and forth through my mind	be - hind a cig - a - rette.	
that ain't what you want to hear,	but that's what I'll do.	
words are gon - na bleed from me	and I will think no more.	

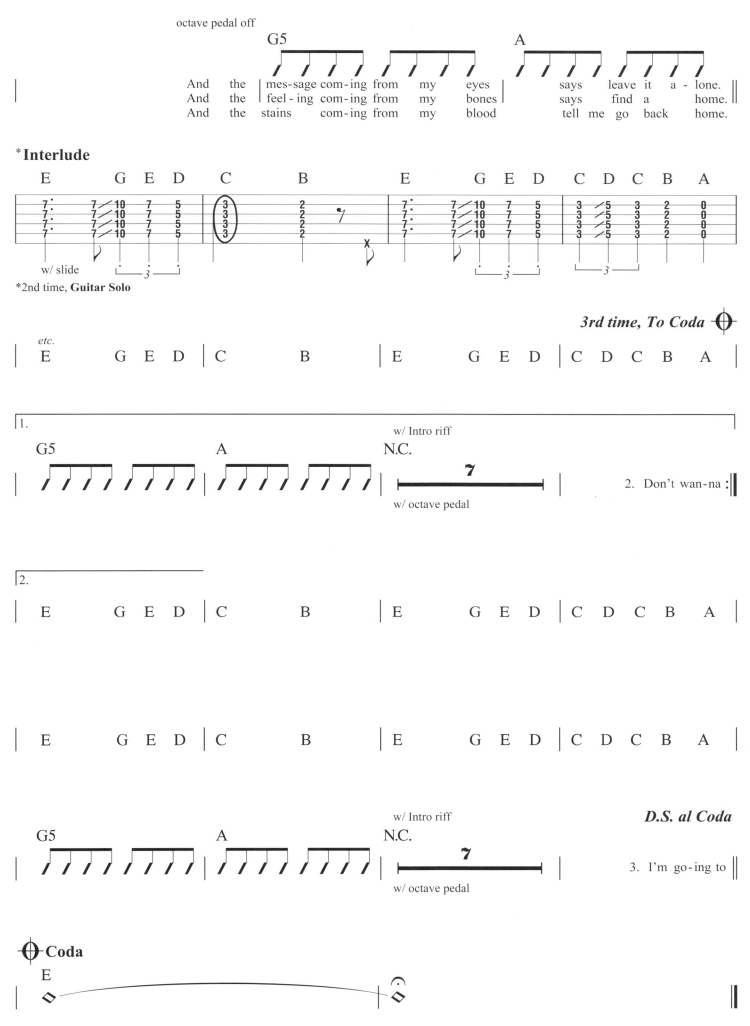

octave pedal off

And the mes-sage com-ing from my eyes says leave it a - lone.
And the feel-ing com-ing from my bones says find a home.
And the stains com-ing from my blood tell me go back home.

*Interlude

w/ slide

*2nd time, **Guitar Solo**

3rd time, To Coda

etc.

1.

w/ Intro riff

w/ octave pedal

2. Don't wan-na

2.

w/ Intro riff

D.S. al Coda

w/ octave pedal

3. I'm go-ing to

Coda

Should I Stay or Should I Go

Words and Music by Mick Jones and Joe Strummer

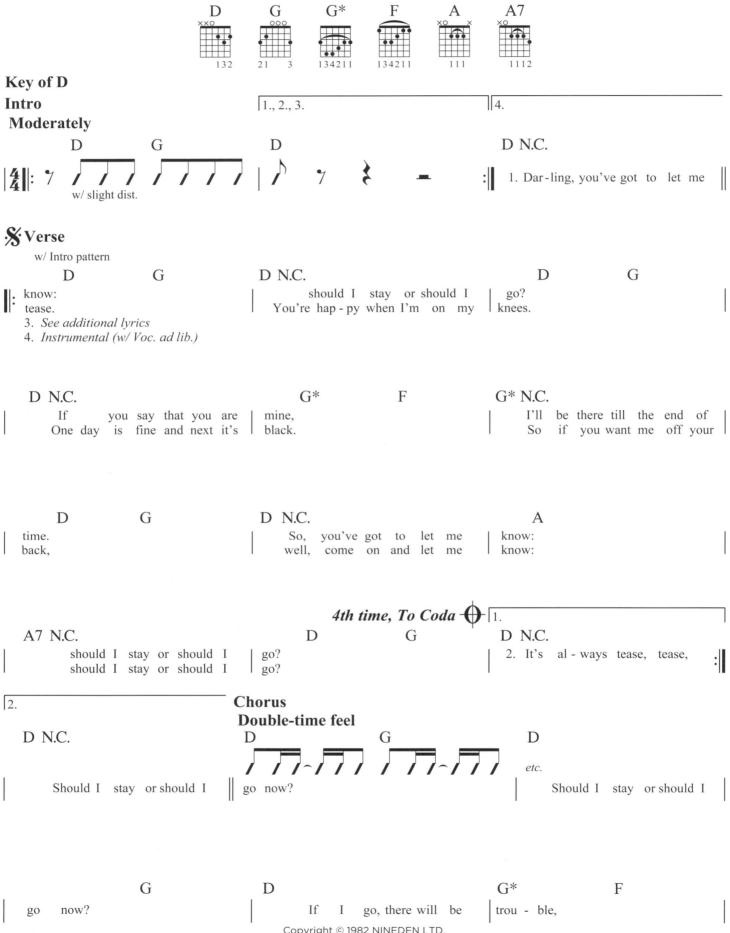

G*   D   G   D

and if I stay, it will be | dou - ble.   So, come on and let me |

End double-time feel

A7   D   G   D   ***D.S. al Coda***
(take repeat)

know.   3. This in - de - ci - sion's bug - gin' ‖

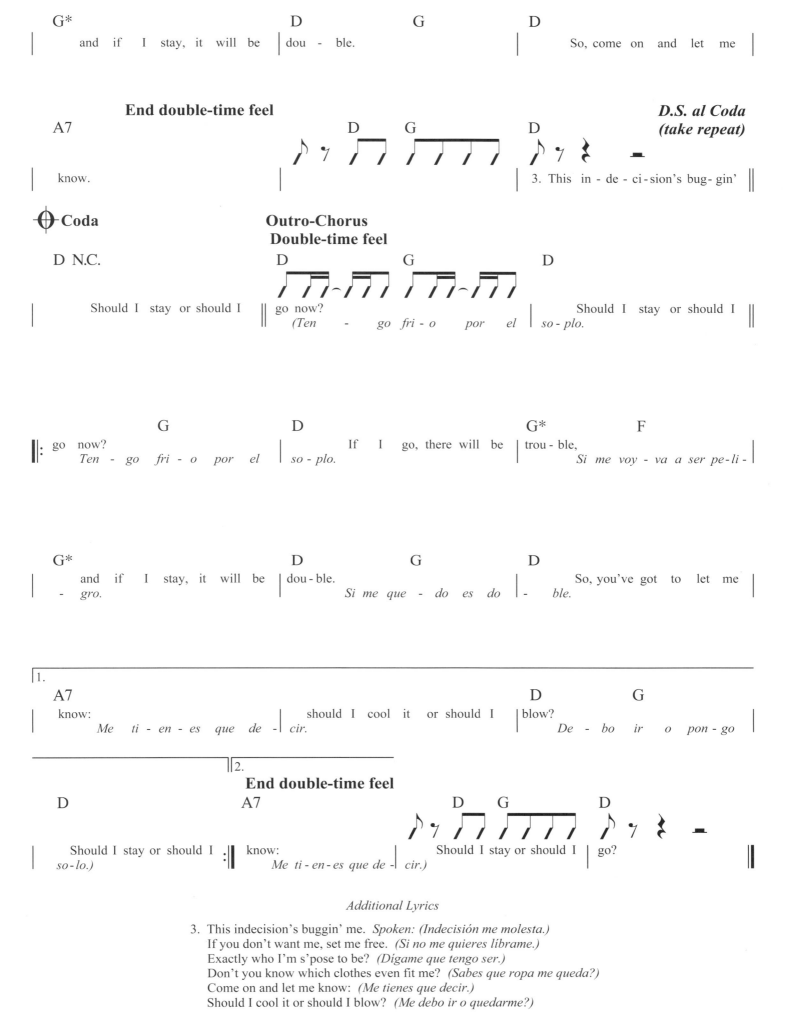

Coda   **Outro-Chorus**
Double-time feel

D N.C.   D   G   D

Should I stay or should I ‖ go now?   Should I stay or should I ‖
(Ten - go fri - o por el | *so - plo.*

G   D   G*   F

‖: go now?   If I go, there will be | trou - ble,
Ten - go fri - o por el | *so - plo.*   *Si me voy - va a ser pe - li -*

G*   D   G   D

and if I stay, it will be | dou - ble.   So, you've got to let me |
- gro.   *Si me que - do es do* | *- ble.*

1.

A7   D   G

know: should I cool it or should I | blow? |
Me ti - en - es que de - | *cir.*   *De - bo ir o pon - go*

2.

End double-time feel

D   A7   D   G   D

Should I stay or should I :‖ know: Should I stay or should I | go?   ‖
so - lo.)   *Me ti - en - es que de -* | *cir.)*

Additional Lyrics

3. This indecision's buggin' me. *Spoken: (Indecisión me molesta.)*
If you don't want me, set me free. *(Si no me quieres líbrame.)*
Exactly who I'm s'pose to be? *(Dígame que tengo ser.)*
Don't you know which clothes even fit me? *(Sabes que ropa me queda?)*
Come on and let me know: *(Me tienes que decir.)*
Should I cool it or should I blow? *(Me debo ir o quedarme?)*

Simple Man

Words and Music by Ronnie Van Zant and Gary Rossington

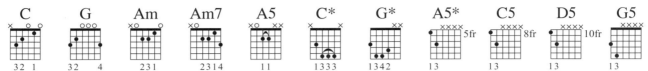

Tune down 1/2 step:
(low to high) Eb-Ab-Db-Gb-Bb-Eb

Key of C

Intro

Slow

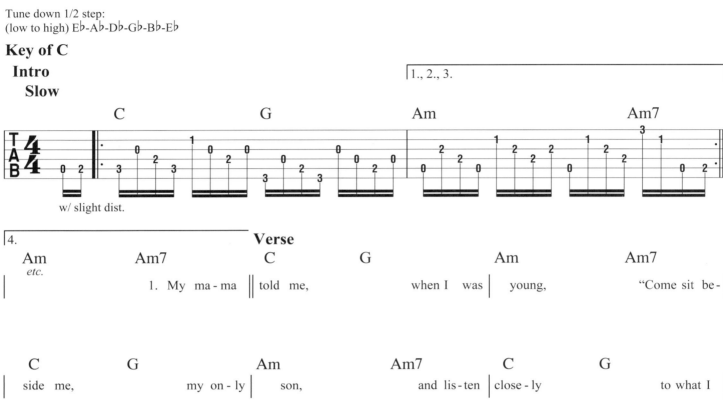

w/ slight dist.

Verse

Am   Am7   C   G   Am   Am7
etc.
                    1. My ma-ma ‖ told me,   when I was | young,   "Come sit be- |

C   G   Am   Am7   C   G
| side me,   my on-ly | son,   and lis-ten | close-ly   to what I |

Am   Am7   C   G   Am   Am7
| say.   And if you | do this,   it-'ll help you   some | sun-ny day."   Ah, yeah. ‖

𝄌 **Interlude**

C   G   Am   Am7

Verse
w/ Intro riff

C   G   Am   Am7   C   G
etc.
                              2. "Oh, take your ‖: time,   don't live |
                              3., 4. *See additional lyrics*

Am   Am7   C   G   Am   Am7
| too fast.   Trou-bles will | come,   and they will | pass.   Go find a |

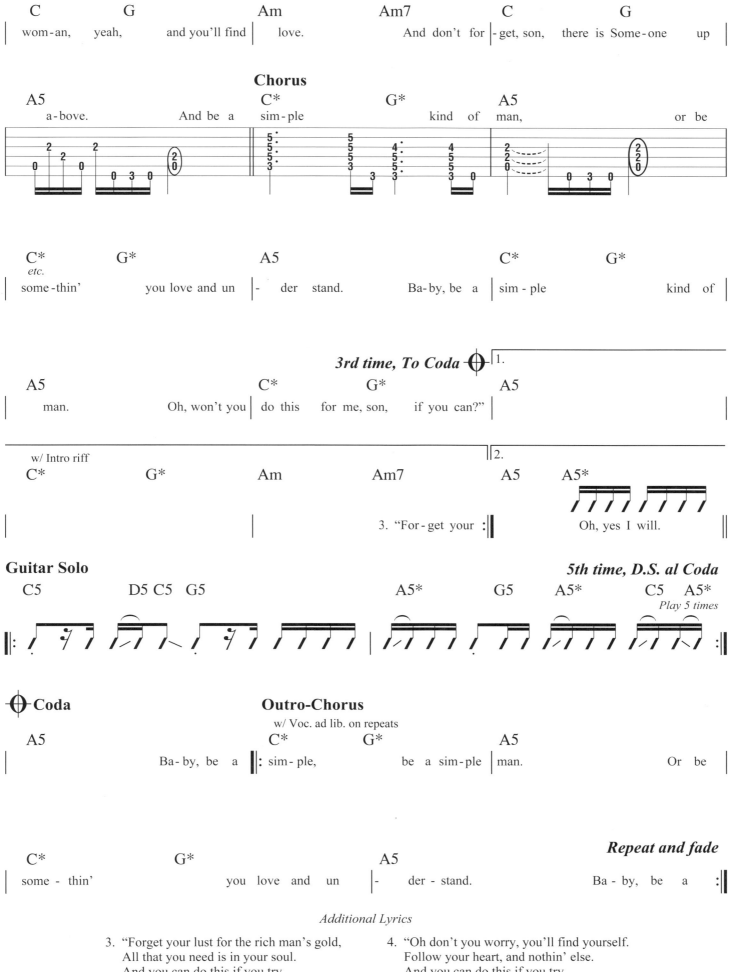

Chorus

3rd time, To Coda

w/ Intro riff

Guitar Solo

5th time, D.S. al Coda

Play 5 times

Coda   Outro-Chorus

w/ Voc. ad lib. on repeats

Repeat and fade

Additional Lyrics

3. "Forget your lust for the rich man's gold,
   All that you need is in your soul.
   And you can do this if you try.
   All that I want for you, my son,
   Is to be satisfied."

4. "Oh don't you worry, you'll find yourself.
   Follow your heart, and nothin' else.
   And you can do this if you try.
   All that I want for you, my son,
   Is to be satisfied."

Smells Like Teen Spirit

Words and Music by Kurt Cobain, Krist Novoselic and Dave Grohl

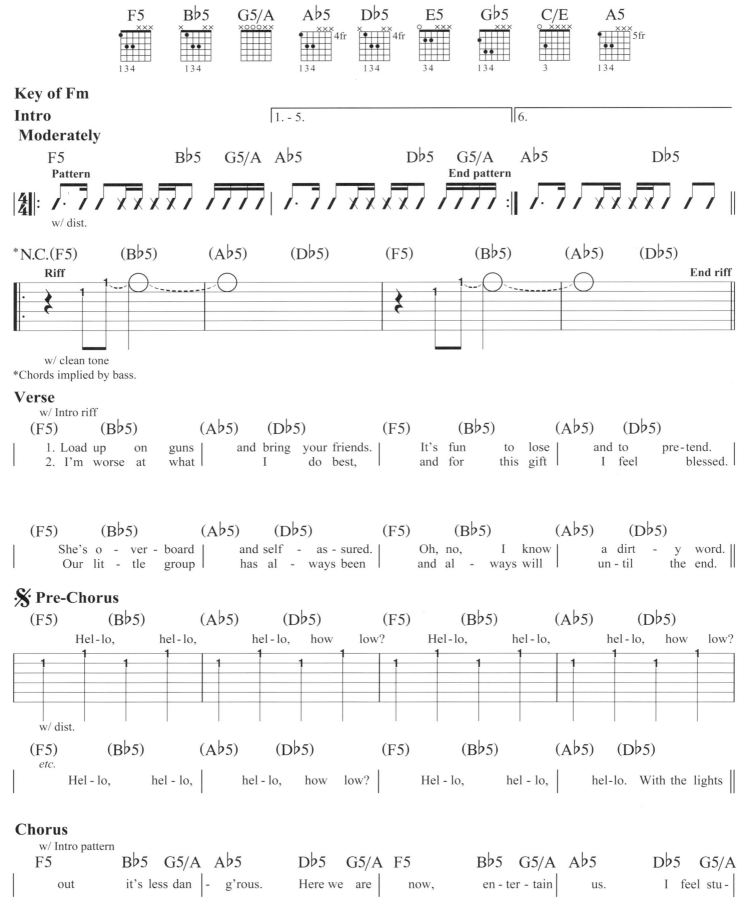

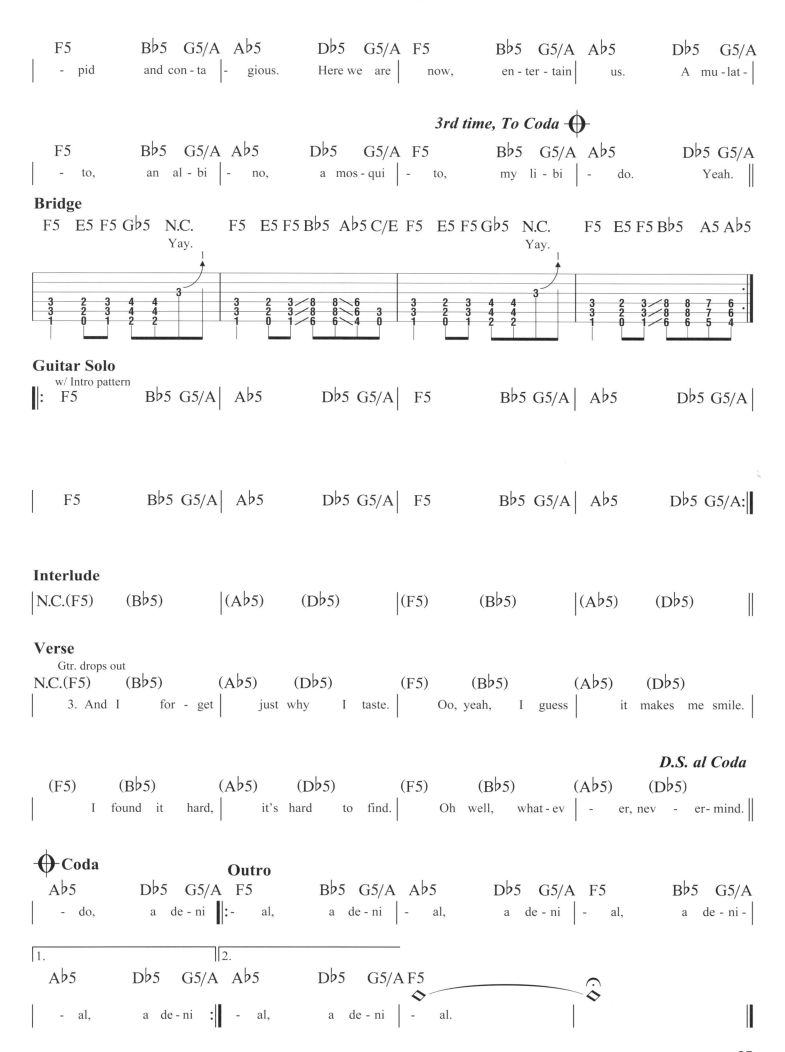

Smoke on the Water

Words and Music by Ritchie Blackmore, Ian Gillan, Roger Glover, Jon Lord and Ian Paice

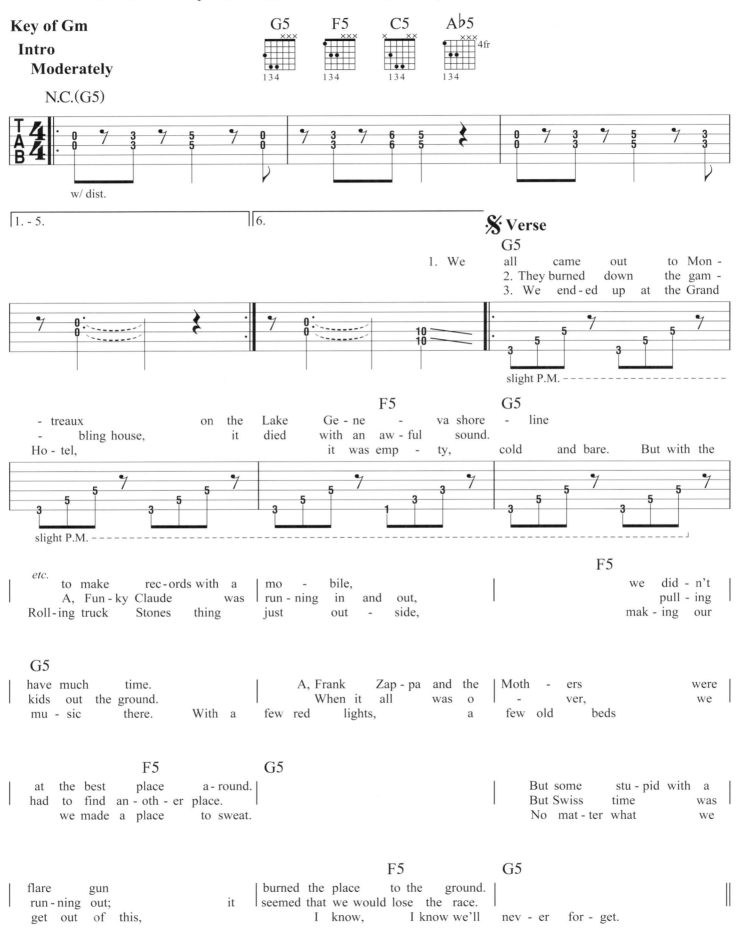

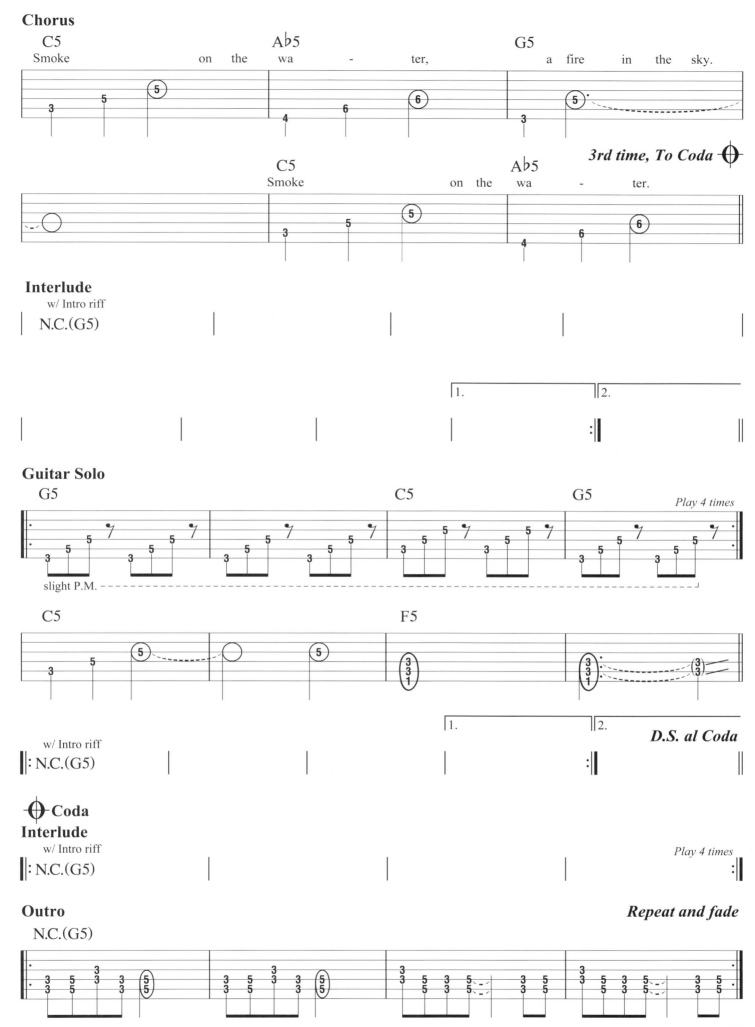

Sunshine of Your Love

Words and Music by Eric Clapton, Jack Bruce and Pete Brown

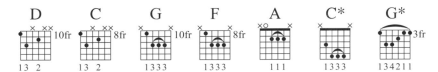

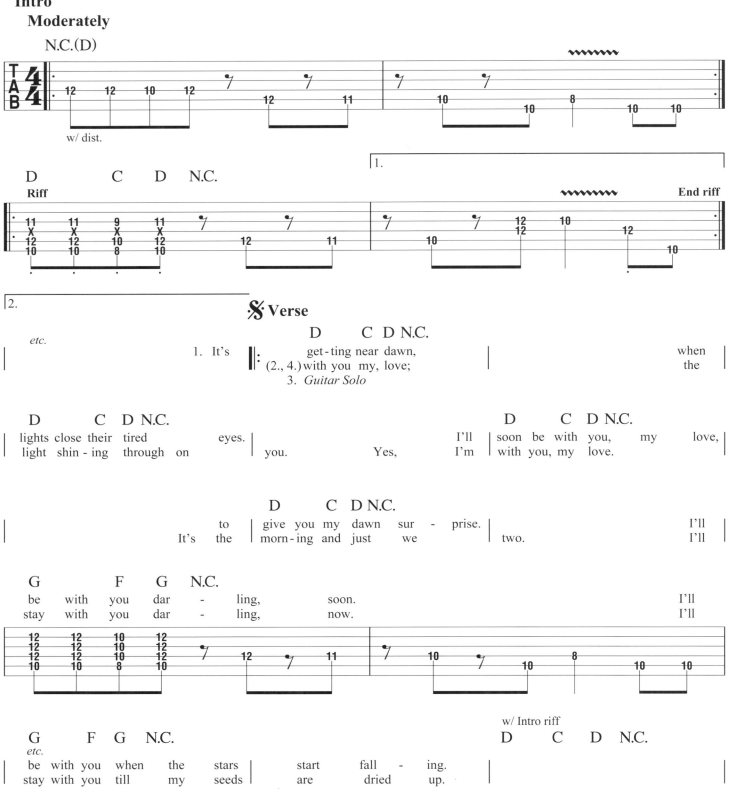

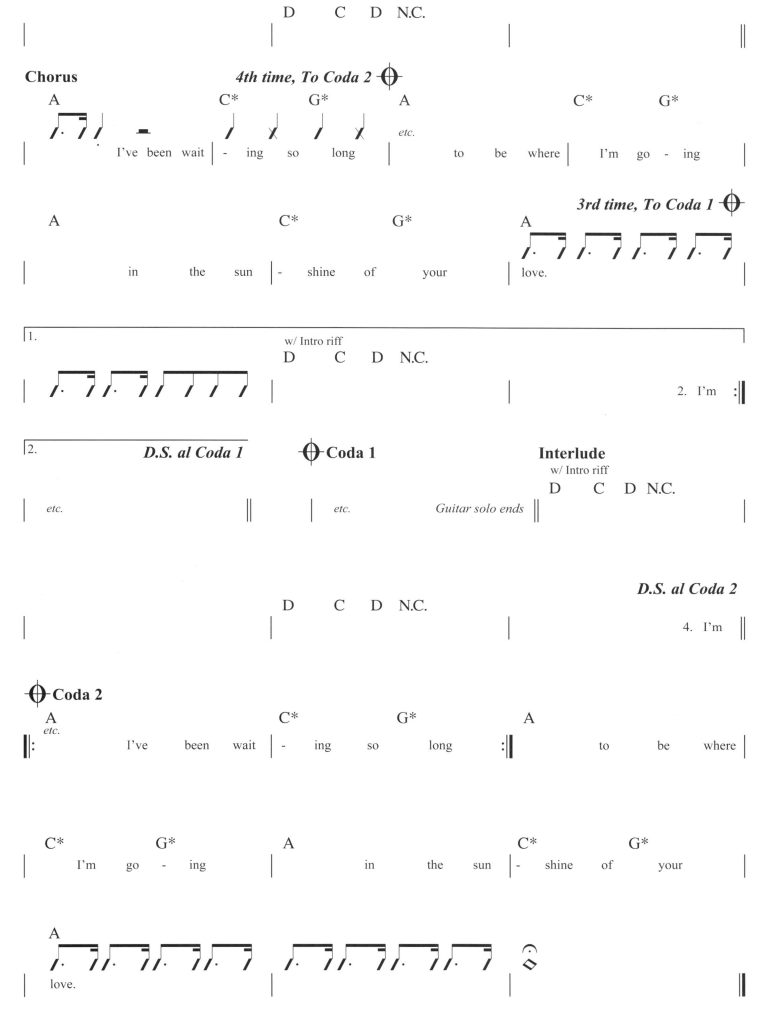

Ticket to Ride

Words and Music by John Lennon and Paul McCartney

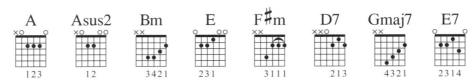

Key of A
Intro
Moderately

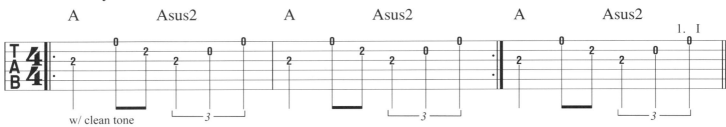

w/ clean tone

Verse

A   Asus2   A   Asus2   A   Asus2

etc.
(3.) think I'm gon-na be sad,   I think it's to-day,   yeah!
(4.) said that liv-ing with me   is bring-in' her down,   yeah!

A   Asus2   A   Asus2   A   Asus2

The | girl that's driv-in' me mad   is go-in' a-way.
She would nev-er be free   when I was a-round.

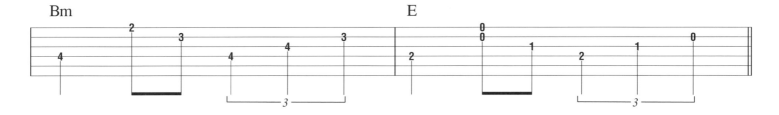

Chorus

F#m   D7   F#m

She's got a tick-et to ride,   she's got a tick-et to ri-

*--
*ride

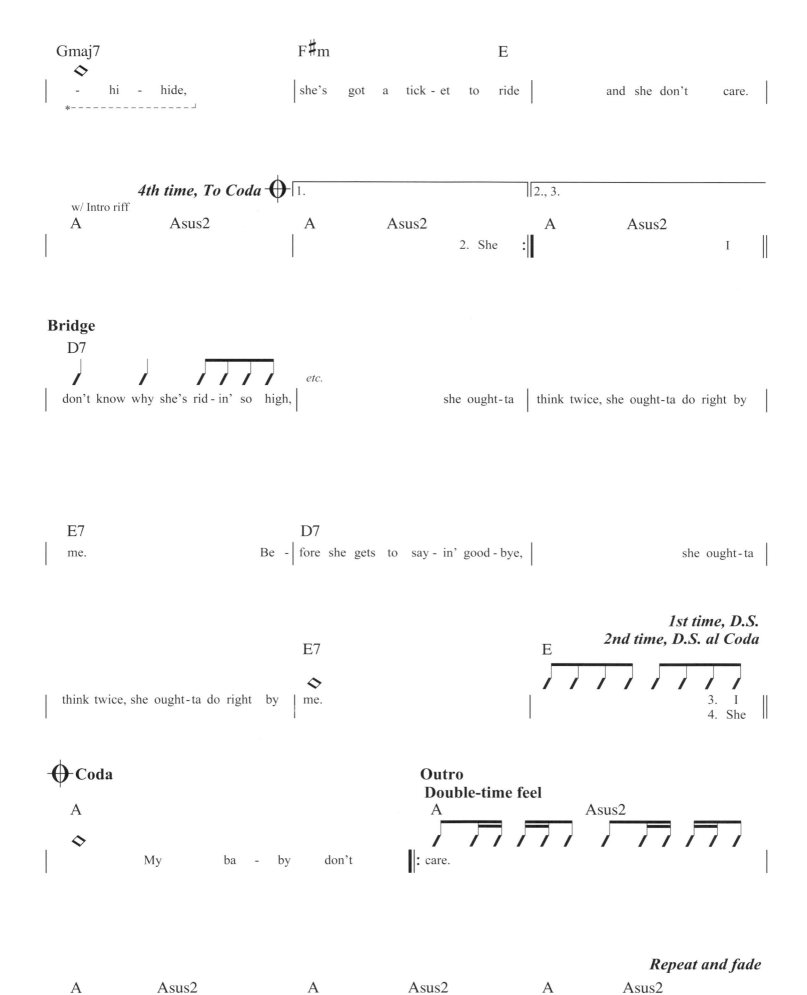

Tube Snake Boogie

Words and Music by Billy F Gibbons, Dusty Hill and Frank Beard

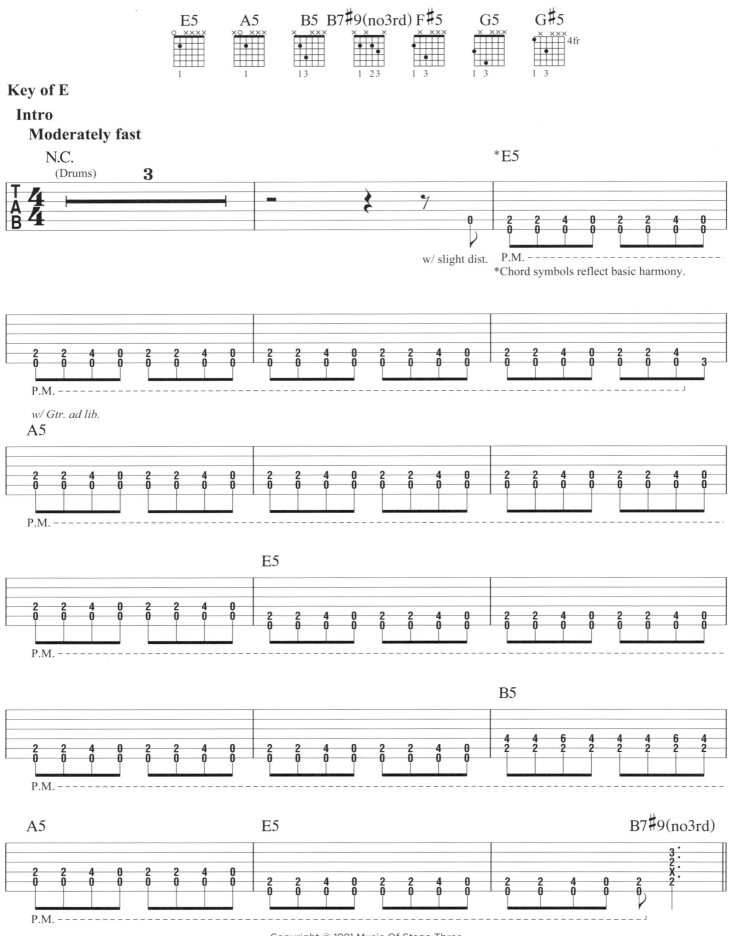

Verse

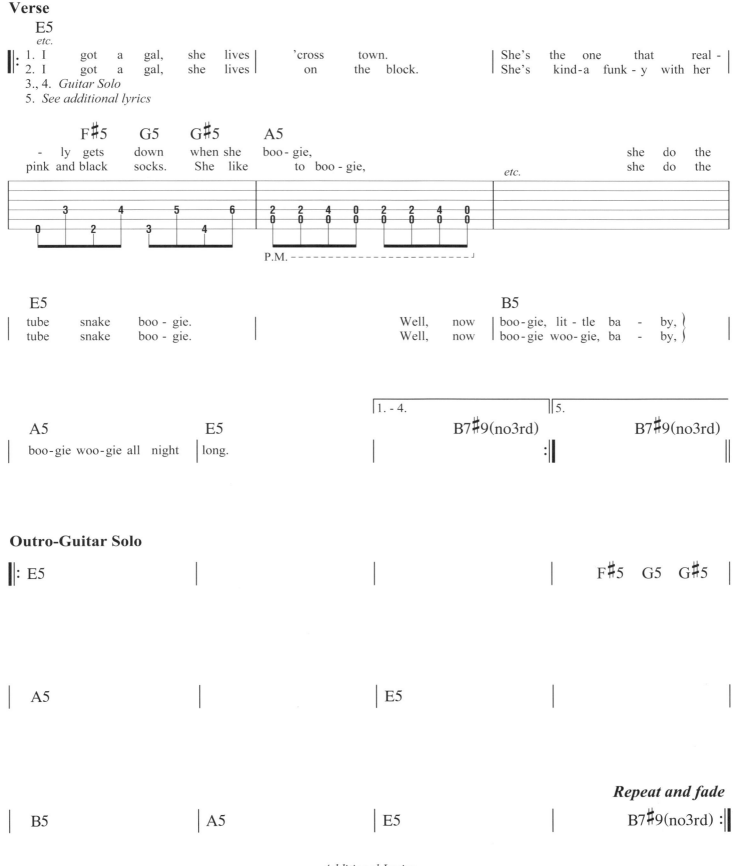

E5
etc.

1. I got a gal, she lives | 'cross town. | She's the one that real -
2. I got a gal, she lives | on the block. | She's kind-a funk-y with her

3., 4. *Guitar Solo*
5. *See additional lyrics*

F#5 G5 G#5 A5

- ly gets down when she boo - gie, | she do the
pink and black socks. She like to boo - gie, *etc.* she do the

P.M. -

E5

tube snake boo - gie. |
tube snake boo - gie. |

B5

Well, now | boo - gie, lit - tle ba - by, }
Well, now | boo - gie woo - gie, ba - by, }

A5   E5

| boo - gie woo - gie all night | long.

1. - 4.
B7#9(no3rd)

5.
B7#9(no3rd)

Outro-Guitar Solo

‖: E5 | | | F#5 G5 G#5 |

| A5 | | E5 | |

Repeat and fade

| B5 | A5 | E5 | B7#9(no3rd) :‖

Additional Lyrics

5. I got a gal, she lives on the hill.
   She won't do it but her sister will.
   When she boogie,
   She do the tube snake boogie.
   Well, now boogie, little baby,
   Boogie woogie all night long.
   Blow your top, blow your top.

Walk Don't Run

By Johnny Smith

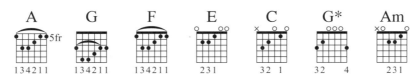

Key of C

Fast

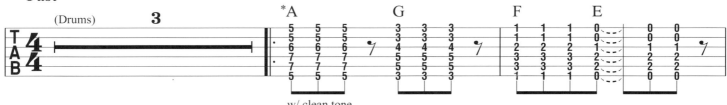

w/ clean tone

*Editor's note: Common practice substitutes Am for the A chord.

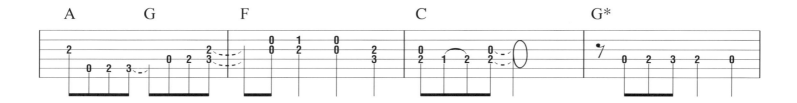

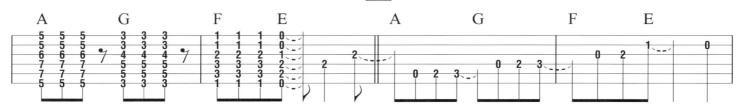

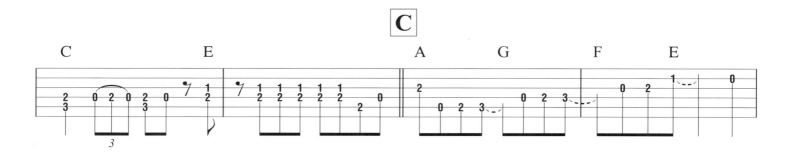

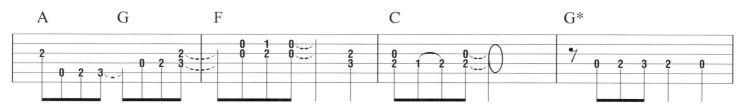

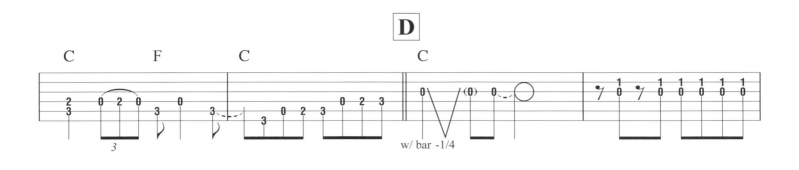

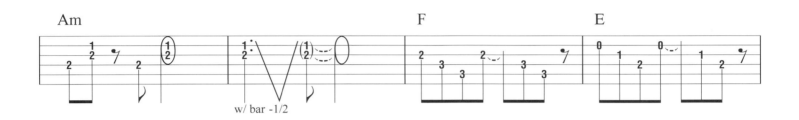

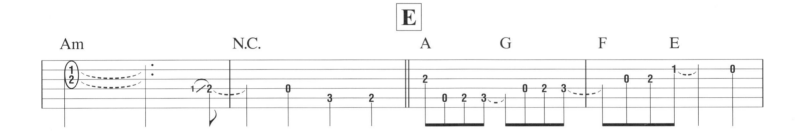

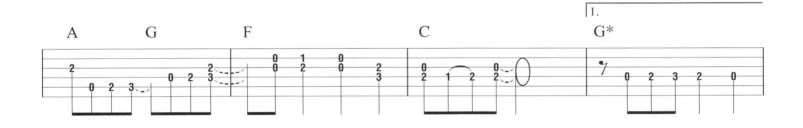

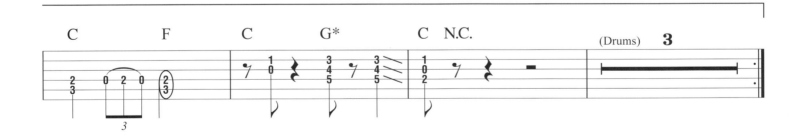

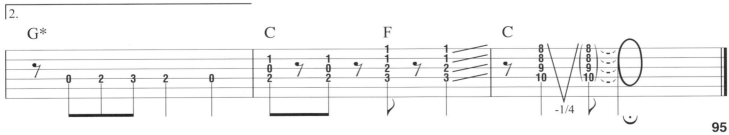

When I Come Around

Words by Billie Joe
Music by Green Day

Tune down 1/2 step:
(low to high) E♭-A♭-D♭-G♭-B♭-E♭

G5   D5   E5   C5   A5

Key of G
Intro
Moderately

N.C.   G5   D5   E5   C5   *Play 3 times*

 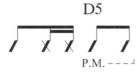   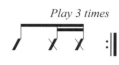

w/ dist.   P.M. - - - ⌐   P.M. - - - ⌐   P.M.

Verse

G5   D5   E5   C5
etc.

1. Well, I   heard   you   cry - in'   loud
2. Well, I   heard   it   all   be - fore,

G5   D5   E5   C5

all   the   way   a - cross   town.   You've   been   search -
so   don't   knock   down   my   door.   I'm   a   los -

G5   D5   E5   C5

- ing   for   that   some - one,   and   it's   me   out   on   the   prowl,   as
- er   and   a   us - er   so   I   don't   need   no   ac - cus - er   to

G5   D5   E5   C5

you   sit   a - round   feel - ing   sor - ry   for   your - self.
try   and   slag   me   down   be - cause   I   know   you're   right.

G5   D5   E5   C5

Well, don't   get   lone - ly   now,
So   go   do   what   you   like.

G5   D5   E5   C5

and   dry   your   whin - ing   eyes.   I'm   just   roam -
Make   sure   you   do   it   wise.   You   might   find

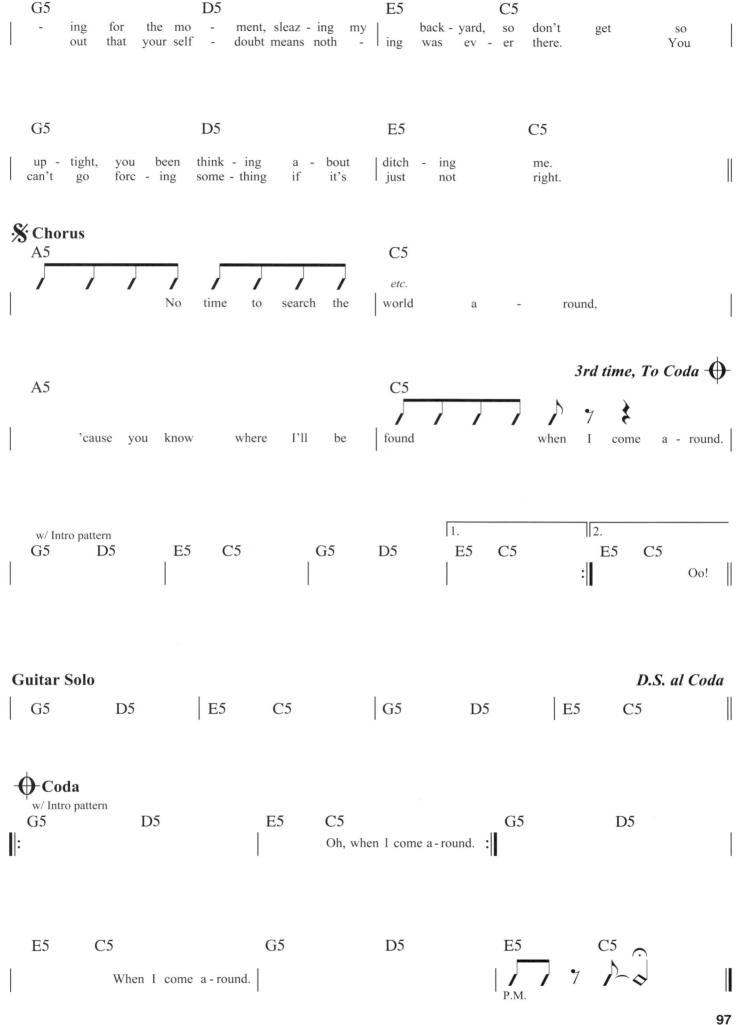

Wild Thing

Words and Music by Chip Taylor

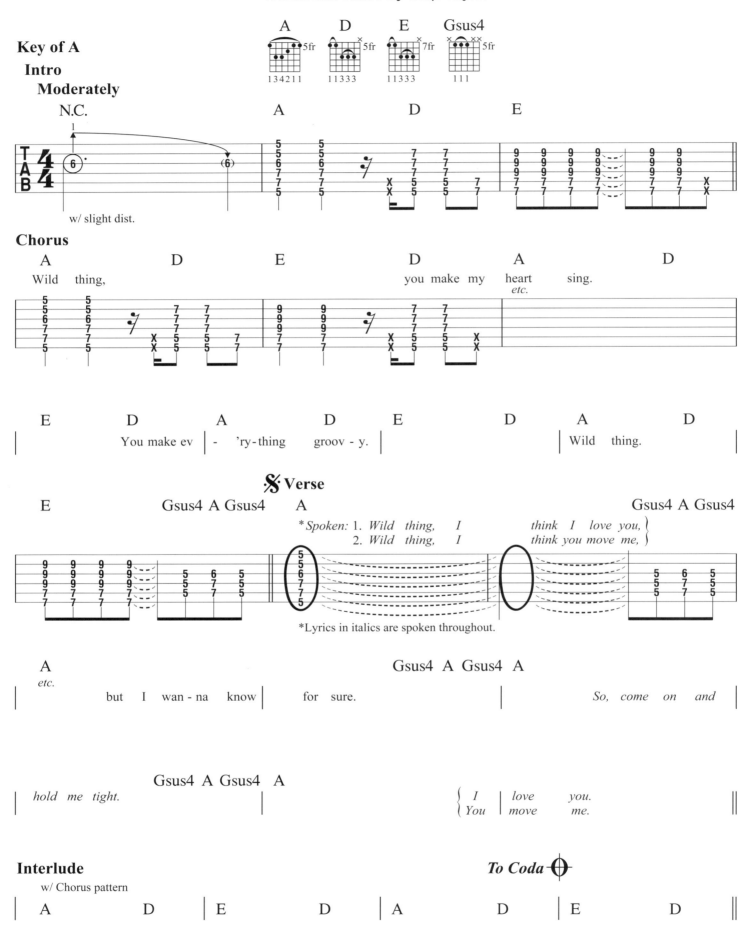

Chorus

w/ Chorus pattern

A	D	E	D	A	D	E	D
Wild thing,			you make my	heart sing.			You make ev-

A	D	E	D	A	D	E
- 'ry-thing groov - y.				Wild thing.		

Recorder Solo

A	D	E	D	A	D	E	D

D.S. al Coda

A	D	E	D	A	D	E	Gsus4 A Gsus4

⊕ Coda

E
etc.

Chorus

w/ Chorus pattern

A	D	E	D	A	D	E	D
Wild thing,			you make my	heart sing.			You make ev-

A	D	E	D	A	D	E	D
- 'ry-thing groov - y.				Wild thing.			Come on, come on

Outro

Repeat and fade

w/ Voc. ad lib. on repeats

A	D	E	D	A	D	E	D
‖: wild thing.			Shake it, shake it,	wild thing.			I love you, :‖

You Really Got Me

Words and Music by Ray Davies

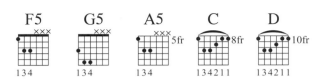

Key of G

Intro

Moderately fast

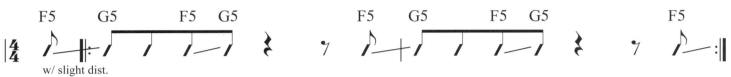

w/ slight dist.

𝄋 Verse

w/ Intro pattern

G5	F5	G5			F5	G5	F5	G5		F5
1. Girl,			you	real - ly	got	me	go - in',	you	got	me
2., 3. See,			don't	ev - er	set	me	free,	I	al - ways

G5		F5	G5			F5	G5	F5	G5		F5
so	I	don't	know	what	I'm	do - in'	now.			
wan - na	be	by	your	side.						

G5		F5	G5			F5	G5	F5	G5		F5
Yeah, }			you	real - ly	got	me	now,	you	got	me
Girl, }										

G5		F5	G5			F5	G5	F5	G5		
so	I	can't	sleep	at	night.					

A5		G5	A5			G5	A5	G5	A5		G5
							etc.				
Yeah,			you	real - ly	got	me	now,	you	got	me

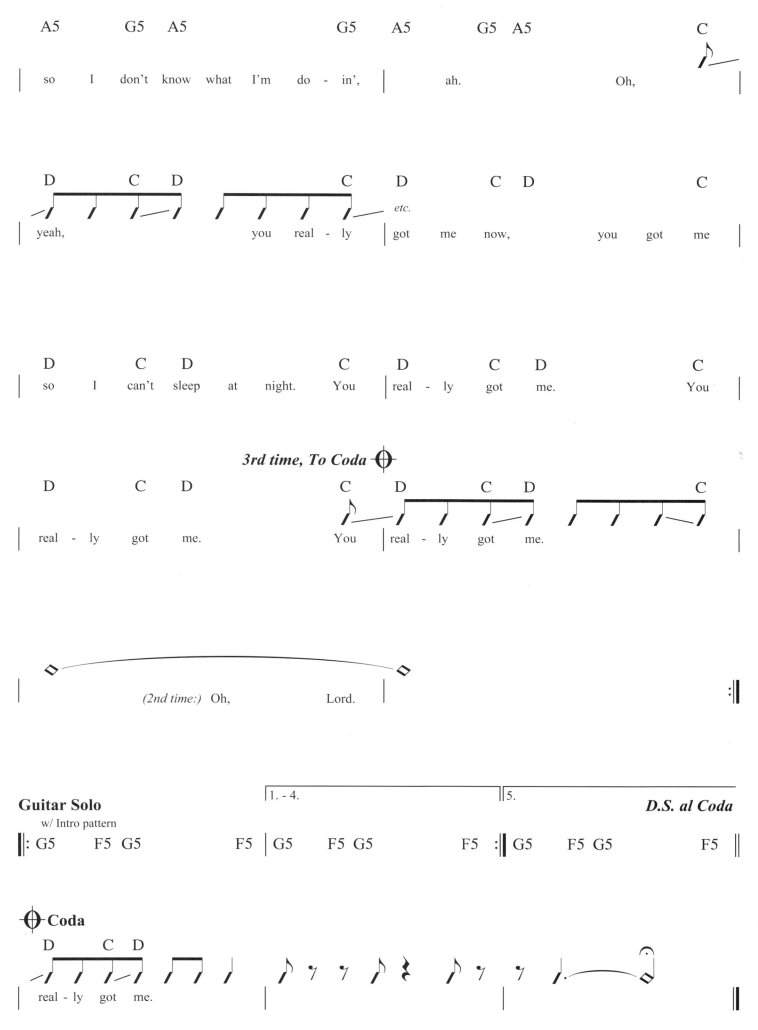

RHYTHM TAB LEGEND

Rhythm Tab is a form of notation that adds rhythmic values to the traditional tab staff.

TABLATURE graphically represents the guitar fingerboard. Each horizontal line represents a string, and each number represents a fret. Rhythmic values are shown using ovals, stems, and dots.

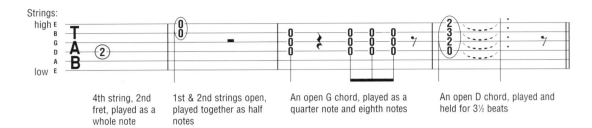

4th string, 2nd fret, played as a whole note

1st & 2nd strings open, played together as half notes

An open G chord, played as a quarter note and eighth notes

An open D chord, played and held for 3½ beats

Definitions for Special Guitar Notation

HALF-STEP BEND: Strike the note and bend up 1/2 step.

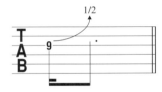

WHOLE-STEP BEND: Strike the note and bend up one step.

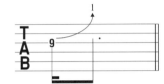

GRACE NOTE BEND: Strike the note and immediately bend up as indicated.

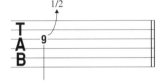

SLIGHT (MICROTONE) BEND: Strike the note and bend up 1/4 step.

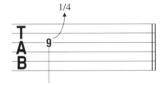

BEND AND RELEASE: Strike the note and bend up as indicated, then release back to the original note. Only the first note is struck.

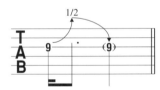

PRE-BEND: Bend the note as indicated, then strike it.

PRE-BEND AND RELEASE: Bend the note as indicated. Strike it and release the bend back to the original note.

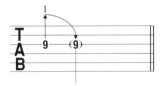

UNISON BEND: Strike the two notes simultaneously and bend the lower note up to the pitch of the higher.

HOLD BEND: While sustaining bent note, strike note on different string.

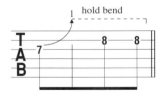

VIBRATO: The string is vibrated by rapidly bending and releasing the note with the fretting hand.

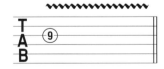

WIDE VIBRATO: The pitch is varied to a greater degree by vibrating with the fretting hand.

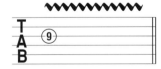

HAMMER-ON: Strike the first (lower) note with one finger, then sound the higher note (on the same string) with another finger by fretting it without picking.

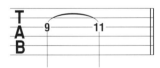

PULL-OFF: Place both fingers on the notes to be sounded. Strike the first note and without picking, pull the finger off to sound the second (lower) note.

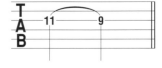

HAMMER FROM NOWHERE: Sound note(s) by hammering with fret hand finger only.

GRACE NOTE SLUR: Strike the note and immediately hammer-on (or pull-off) as indicated.

GRACE NOTE SLUR (CLUSTER): Strike the notes and immediately hammer-on (or pull-off) as indicated.

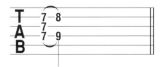

LEGATO SLIDE: Strike the first note and then slide the same fret-hand finger up or down to the second note. The second note is not struck.

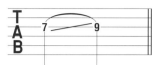

SHIFT SLIDE: Same as legato slide, except the second note is struck.

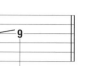

TRILL: Very rapidly alternate between the notes indicated by continuously hammering on and pulling off.

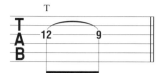

TAPPING: Hammer ("tap") the fret indicated with the pick-hand index or middle finger and pull off to the note fretted by the fret hand.

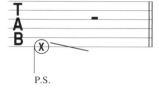

NATURAL HARMONIC: Strike the note while the fret-hand lightly touches the string directly over the fret indicated.

Harm.

PINCH HARMONIC: The note is fretted normally and a harmonic is produced by adding the edge of the thumb or the tip of the index finger of the pick hand to the normal pick attack.

P.H.

HARP HARMONIC: The note is fretted normally and a harmonic is produced by gently resting the pick hand's index finger directly above the indicated fret (in parentheses) while the pick hand's thumb or pick assists by plucking the appropriate string.

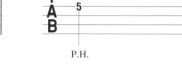

H.H.

PICK SCRAPE: The edge of the pick is rubbed down (or up) the string, producing a scratchy sound.

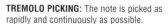

P.S.

MUFFLED STRINGS: A percussive sound is produced by laying the fret hand across the string(s) without depressing, and striking them with the pick hand.

PALM MUTING: The note is partially muted by the pick hand lightly touching the string(s) just before the bridge.

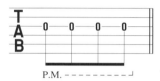

P.M. ---------

RAKE: Drag the pick across the strings indicated with a single motion.

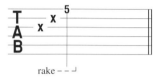

rake - - -

TREMOLO PICKING: The note is picked as rapidly and continuously as possible.

ARPEGGIATE: Play the notes of the chord indicated by quickly rolling them from bottom to top.

VIBRATO BAR DIVE AND RETURN: The pitch of the note or chord is dropped a specified number of steps (in rhythm), then returned to the original pitch.

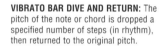
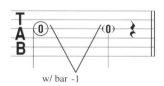

w/ bar -1

VIBRATO BAR SCOOP: Depress the bar just before striking the note, then quickly release the bar.

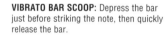
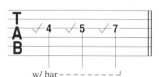

w/ bar - - - - - - - -

VIBRATO BAR DIP: Strike the note and then immediately drop a specified number of steps, then release back to the original pitch.

w/ bar - - - - - - -

Additional Musical Definitions

(accent) • Accentuate note (play it louder)

(staccato) • Play the note short

(fermata) • A hold or pause

⊓ • Downstroke

∨ • Upstroke

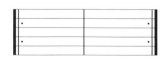

• Repeat measures between signs

NOTE: Tablature numbers in parentheses are used when:
• The note is sustained, but a new articulation begins (such as a hammer-on, pull-off, slide, or bend), or
• A bend is released.

FIRST 50

Books in the First 50 series contain easy to intermediate arrangements for must-know songs.
Each arrangement is simple and streamlined, yet still captures the essence of the tune.

First 50 Baroque Pieces
You Should Play on Guitar
Includes selections by Johann Sebastian Bach, Robert de Visée, Ernst Gottlieb Baron, Santiago de Murcia, Antonio Vivaldi, Sylvius Leopold Weiss, and more.
00322567...$14.99

First 50 Bluegrass Solos
You Should Play on Guitar
I Am a Man of Constant Sorrow • Long Journey Home • Molly and Tenbrooks • Old Joe Clark • Rocky Top • Salty Dog Blues • and more.
00298574...$15.99

First 50 Blues Songs
You Should Play on Guitar
All Your Love (I Miss Loving) • Bad to the Bone • Born Under a Bad Sign • Dust My Broom • Hoodoo Man Blues • Little Red Rooster • Love Struck Baby • Pride and Joy • Smoking Gun • Still Got the Blues • The Thrill Is Gone • You Shook Me • and more.
00235790...$17.99

First 50 Blues Turnarounds
You Should Play on Guitar
You'll learn cool turnarounds in the styles of these jazz legends: John Lee Hooker, Robert Johnson, Joe Pass, Jimmy Rogers, Hubert Sumlin, Stevie Ray Vaughan, T-Bone Walker, Muddy Waters, and more.
00277469...$14.99

First 50 Chords
You Should Play on Guitar
American Pie • Back in Black • Brown Eyed Girl • Landslide • Let It Be • Riptide • Summer of '69 • Take Me Home, Country Roads • Won't Get Fooled Again • You've Got a Friend • and more.
00300255 Guitar.....................................$12.99

First 50 Classical Pieces
You Should Play on Guitar
Includes compositions by J.S. Bach, Augustin Barrios, Matteo Carcassi, Domenico Scarlatti, Fernando Sor, Francisco Tárrega, Robert de Visée, Antonio Vivaldi and many more.
00155414...$15.99

First 50 Folk Songs
You Should Play on Guitar
Amazing Grace • Down by the Riverside • Home on the Range • I've Been Working on the Railroad • Kumbaya • Man of Constant Sorrow • Oh! Susanna • This Little Light of Mine • When the Saints Go Marching In • The Yellow Rose of Texas • and more.
00235868 ....$15.99

First 50 Guitar Duets
You Should Play
Chopsticks • Clocks • Eleanor Rigby • Game of Thrones Theme • Hallelujah • Linus and Lucy (from *A Charlie Brown Christmas*) • Memory (from *Cats*) • Over the Rainbow (from *The Wizard of Oz*) • Star Wars (Main Theme) • What a Wonderful World • You Raise Me Up • and more.
00319706...$14.99

First 50 Jazz Standards
You Should Play on Guitar
All the Things You Are • Body and Soul • Don't Get Around Much Anymore • Fly Me to the Moon (In Other Words) • The Girl from Ipanema (Garota De Ipanema) • I Got Rhythm • Laura • Misty • Night and Day • Satin Summertime • When I Fall in Love • and more.
00198594 Solo Guitar $15.99

First 50 Kids' Songs
You Should Play on Guitar
Do-Re-Mi • Hakuna Matata • Let It Go • My Favorite Things • Puff the Magic Dragon • Take Me Out to the Ball Game • Won't You Be My Neighbor? (It's a Beautiful Day in the Neighborhood) • and more.
00300500 ....$15.99

First 50 Licks
You Should Play on Guitar
Licks presented include the styles of legendary guitarists like Eric Clapton, Buddy Guy, Jimi Hendrix, B.B. King, Randy Rhoads, Carlos Santana, Stevie Ray Vaughan and many more.
00278875 Book/Online Audio...........$14.99

First 50 Riffs
You Should Play on Guitar
All Right Now • Back in Black • Barracuda • Carry on Wayward Son • Crazy Train • La Grange • Layla • Seven Nation Army • Smoke on the Water • Sunday Bloody Sunday • Sunshine of Your Love • Sweet Home Alabama • Working Man • and more.
00277366...$12.99

First 50 Rock Songs You Should
Play on Electric Guitar
All Along the Watchtower • Beat It • Brown Eyed Girl • Cocaine • Detroit Rock City • Hallelujah • (I Can't Get No) Satisfaction • Oh, Pretty Woman • Pride and Joy • Seven Nation Army • Should I Stay or Should I Go • Smells like Teen Spirit • Smoke on the Water • When I Come Around • You Really Got Me • and more.
00131159...$15.99

First 50 Songs by the Beatles You
Should Play on Guitar
All You Need Is Love • Blackbird • Come Together • Eleanor Rigby • Hey Jude • I Want to Hold Your Hand • Let It Be • Ob-La-Di, Ob-La-Da • She Loves You • Twist and Shout • Yellow Submarine • Yesterday • and more.
00295323...$19.99

First 50 Songs
You Should Fingerpick on Guitar
Annie's Song • Blackbird • The Boxer • Classical Gas • Dust in the Wind • Fire and Rain • Greensleeves • Road Trippin' • Shape of My Heart • Tears in Heaven • Time in a Bottle • Vincent (Starry Starry Night) • and more.
00149269...$15.99

First 50 Songs You Should
Play on 12-String Guitar
California Dreamin' • Closer to the Heart • Free Fallin' • Give a Little Bit • Hotel California • Leaving on a Jet Plane • Life by the Drop • Over the Hills and Far Away • Solsbury Hill • Space Oddity • Wish You Were Here • You Wear It Well • and more.
00287559...$15.99

First 50 Songs You Should Play on
Acoustic Guitar
Against the Wind • Boulevard of Broken Dreams • Champagne Supernova • Every Rose Has Its Thorn • Fast Car • Free Fallin' • Layla • Let Her Go • Mean • One • Ring of Fire • Signs • Stairway to Heaven • Trouble • Wagon Wheel • Yellow • Yesterday • and more.
00131209...$15.99

First 50 Songs
You Should Play on Bass
Blister in the Sun • I Got You (I Feel Good) • Livin' on a Prayer • Low Rider • Money • Monkey Wrench • My Generation • Roxanne • Should I Stay or Should I Go • Uptown Funk • What's Going On • With or Without You • Yellow • and more.
00149189 ....$15.99

First 50 Songs
You Should Play on Solo Guitar
Africa • All of Me • Blue Skies • California Dreamin' • Change the World • Crazy • Dream a Little Dream of Me • Every Breath You Take • Hallelujah • Wonderful Tonight • Yesterday • You Raise Me Up • Your Song • and more.
00288843...$16.99

First 50 Songs
You Should Strum on Guitar
American Pie • Blowin' in the Wind • Daughter • Hey, Soul Sister • Home • I Will Wait • Losing My Religion • Mrs. Robinson • No Woman No Cry • Peaceful Easy Feeling • Rocky Mountain High • Sweet Caroline • Teardrops on My Guitar • Wonderful Tonight • and more.
00148996 Guitar.....................................$15.99

HAL•LEONARD®
www.halleonard.com

0421
014